The Power and Practice of the Church

God, Discipleship, and Ministry

John P. Lathrop

The Power and Practice of the Church: God, Discipleship, and Ministry

Copyright © 2010 John P. Lathrop. All rights reserved.

Published by J. Timothy King.
http://www.JTimothyKing.com/

First trade paperback edition, October 2010.
Printed in the United States of America.

ISBN 978-0-9816925-5-5

10   9   8   7   6   5   4   3   2   1

Dedication

This book is dedicated to two men who have been instrumental in teaching me to think as I have studied the Bible, Rev. John King and Rev. Nat Saginario.

Table of Contents

Acknowledgements

I would like to thank Rev. John Tedesco, Director of Publications for the International Fellowship of Christian Assemblies, and Raul Mock, Executive Editor of the Pneuma Review, for giving me their blessing to include some of the material in this book that was previously published in their publications. I would also like to thank my copy editors my wife, Cynthia, and our friend, Esmé Bieberly. Thanks also go to Joshua Paul King for creating the cover.

Preface

This book is a collection of articles that I have written over the years. Some of the articles were originally written as seminary assignments (Chapters 1, 2, 3, 7, 8, 9, 13, 14); some are adaptations of sermons that I have preached (Chapters 11, 12, 15); and some were written originally for publication in *Vista Magazine* (Chapters 4, 5, 6, 10, 16, 17, 18), the official publication of the Christian Church of North America, now known as the International Fellowship of Christian Assemblies. I have made some minor revisions to some of the material. A couple of the articles have been published by both *Vista Magazine* and the Pneuma Foundation. The articles cover a number of different subjects, but basically they center on three themes: God, discipleship, and ministry. I hope that you will find the contents of this book to be both instructive and inspirational.

John P. Lathrop

May 2010

Chapter 1   Tongues: The Controversial Gift

The twentieth century has witnessed the rapid growth of two remarkable religious movements, the Pentecostal Movement and the Charismatic Movement. The Pentecostal Movement, which appeared first, attracted widespread attention in the early 1900s. This was due largely to the revival services that took place at the Azusa Street Mission in Los Angeles beginning in 1906.[1] A little more than fifty years later the Charismatic Movement burst on the scene claiming the same spiritual manifestations that had previously appeared in the Pentecostal Movement. The Charismatic Renewal, sometimes called neo-pentecostalism, began to make its way into the mainline Protestant churches in the late 1950s, and by 1967 had infiltrated the Roman Catholic Church as well.[2] The impact of these movements has been profound. The sheer number of people involved indicates that. In 1995 the number of adherents to the Pentecostal Movement was said to be 410 million.[3] These movements have touched the world. While there are differences between the two movements, the one thing that they hold in common is the claim to fresh outpourings of the Holy Spirit, complete with healings and the other gifts of the Spirit, including the gift of tongues.

The gift of tongues, referred to by the apostle Paul in First Corinthians

---

[1] Stanley Burgess and Gary McGee, eds. *Dictionary of Pentecostal and Charismatic Movements* (Grand Rapids, MI: Zondervan, 1988), s.v. "Azusa Street Revival," by C.M. Robeck Jr.

[2] Charles E. Hummel, *Fire in the Fireplace: Contemporary Charismatic Renewal* (Downers Grove, IL: InterVarsity Press, 1978), 39.

[3] Harvey Cox, *Fire From Heaven: The Rise of Pentecostal Spirituality and the Reshaping of Religion in the Twenty-first Century* (Reading, MA: Addison-Wesley Publishing, 1995), xv.

chapters 12-14, is perhaps the most controversial of the gifts of the Spirit. The reported reappearance of this gift in the Pentecostal and Charismatic Movements has produced responses ranging from joy to horror. The purpose of this article is to consider the controversy regarding this gift, examine the contribution that the gift can make to the church, and contend for the restoration of this gift to its rightful place in the life of the church.

In dealing with this subject I will focus primarily on Paul's teaching concerning the gift in his first epistle to the Corinthians. Although speaking in tongues is mentioned in the Book of Acts, I will not include it in this article because it seems to be somewhat different from the gift described by Paul in First Corinthians. In Acts, more than one person can speak at a time, and no interpretation appears to be required.[4] I will restrict my treatment of the subject to the gift proper, which is for congregational use and requires interpretation.

The major controversy regarding the gift of tongues concerns its existence. The Christian Church today is divided on the issue of whether this gift exists in our day or not. Christians who believe that the gift of tongues still exists are called Charismatics or Pentecostals. Christians who do not believe that the gift exists today are called cessationists.

Regardless of one's theological or denominational persuasion, one thing that must be admitted about the gift is that it did exist in the first-century church. The apostle Paul makes repeated reference to it in First Corinthians chapters 12 and 14. No other New Testament epistle makes any direct reference to this gift. However, this is not to suggest that the gift was something unique to the church at Corinth. The cessationist Benjamin B. Warfield believed that the gift existed in the apostolic church and that it was not limited to Corinth.[5] In fact he goes so far as to say that an apostolic church

---

[4] Carl Brumback, *What Meaneth This?* (Springfield, MO: Gospel Publishing House, 1947), 268-269.

[5] Benjamin B. Warfield, *Counterfeit Miracles* (New York: Charles Scribner's Sons, 1918), 5.

without the gifts would be an exception.[6] The gifts, including tongues, were a regular part of church life in the first century.

The Christians at Corinth were very much people of the Spirit. As Paul writes to them, they are already experiencing the gifts of the Holy Spirit. Paul said that they did not lack any spiritual gift (1 Cor. 1:7). This was certainly true of the gift of tongues. The amount of space given to it in First Corinthians 14 makes that clear. The gift of tongues held a prominent place in the Corinthian assembly even though it was not a gift for all (1 Cor. 12:30). As others have pointed out, it is significant to note that in all of his instructions regarding tongues Paul never speaks of it in a derogatory way. However, he does lay down some guidelines concerning the proper expression of the gift. This is not because there is anything wrong with the gift, but because the Corinthians were not using it correctly. They seem to have exercised it without restraint or interpretation. Paul's correction of the Corinthians' errors provides us with the most extensive information anywhere in Scripture concerning the gift's nature and function.

The scriptural teaching that Paul gives concerning the gift affirms a number of significant things about it. The first concerns its source. In First Corinthians 12 he repeatedly emphasizes that the gifts come from God (1 Cor. 12:4, 8-11). The second important point that he brings out is the purpose of the gift. The purpose of the gift of tongues, and all of the other gifts of the Spirit, is edification (1 Cor. 14:5,26). That is, the gifts are meant to build up and strengthen the church. It is God's intention that they make a positive contribution to the health and well-being of the church. The third important point that Paul makes concerns the permanency of the gift. It is true that Scripture says that tongues will be stilled (1 Cor. 13:8). The context indicates that this will happen when we see Christ face to face.[7] Thus, the gifts, including tongues, are a part of the church age and will continue until Christ

---

[6] Ibid.

[7] Douglas A. Oss, "A Charismatic/Pentecostal View," *Are Miraculous Gifts for Today?* ed. Wayne A. Grudem, Counterpoints (Grand Rapids, MI: Zondervan, 1996), 274.

returns. This truth is also affirmed in First Corinthians 1:7 where Paul says that the Corinthians lack no spiritual gift as they wait for Christ to be revealed.[8]

While there can be no argument that the gift of tongues existed in the apostolic church, there are those in the contemporary church who do not believe that this gift exists today. They believe that the gift is no longer given (1 Cor. 13:8). The people who hold this view are known as cessationists. Their theological position is built upon a combination of historical observation and scriptural interpretation.

Benjamin B. Warfield is one of the better-known cessationists. His book, *Counterfeit Miracles*, first appeared a little more than a decade after the Pentecostal Movement was launched from Azusa Street. In this book he argues that the gifts have passed away.[9] But as cessationist Richard B. Gaffin Jr. points out, Warfield's defense of the cessationist position rests predominantly upon historical rather than exegetical evidence.[10] Warfield notes the experience of the post-apostolic church and some of the teachings of early church leaders.[11] Since their combined testimony seems to indicate that the gifts had largely passed from the scene, Warfield sees this as confirmation of the fact that the gifts have ceased. Some cessationists, however, allow for the continuation of the gifts up until the third or fourth century.[12] Warfield is more radical, for he maintains that the gifts were the possession of the apostles and could not be conferred without them.[13] This would greatly limit the distribution of the gifts. What is interesting about the cessationists' position is that logic and experience rather than revelation become the measuring stick of truth. It is also ironic since the cessationists sometimes charge Charis-

---

[8] Ibid.

[9] Warfield, 3-31.

[10] Richard B. Gaffin, Jr., "A Cessationist View," *Are Miraculous Gifts for Today?* ed. Wayne A. Grudem, Counterpoints (Grand Rapids, MI: Zondervan, 1996), 28.

[11] Warfield, 5-31.

[12] Ibid., 6-12.

[13] Ibid., 6, 23.

matics and Pentecostals with interpreting Scripture by experience. Here we see that they too can be charged with the same thing.[14]

However, the cessationists do also offer a scriptural foundation for their position. One text that they appeal to is First Corinthians 13:8-9. This text specifically says that tongues will be stilled when perfection comes. A cessationist interpretation of the text is that the perfection to come is the completion of the canon.[15] As was stated earlier, the context of First Corinthians 13 does not support this interpretation. Noted textual critic Gordon Fee dismisses the cessationist interpretation of this text, not only on the basis of context, but also on the grounds of Paul's intention and the recipients' understanding.[16] He maintains that Paul couldn't have meant the completion of the canon and that the Corinthians couldn't have understood him to be saying this.[17]

Cessationist John F. MacArthur Jr. offers another scriptural argument for the passing of the gifts. In his book, *Charismatic Chaos*, he asserts that the last record of miraculous gifts in the New Testament took place in A.D. 58.[18] He also says that tongues are not mentioned in any of the later books of the New Testament.[19] This is the argument from silence, which is never really conclusive or convincing. As ex-cessationist Jack Deere has pointed out, the cessationist position is not one that naturally comes from Scripture; it is a position that one has to be taught.[20]

Those who believe in the present-day existence of the gift of tongues do not necessarily agree about what the contents of an utterance in tongues

---

[14] Gordon D. Fee, *Gospel and Spirit: Issues in New Testament Hermeneutics* (Peabody, MA: Hendrickson Publishers, 1991), 119.

[15] Jack Deere, *Surprised by the Power of the Spirit* (Grand Rapids, MI: Zondervan, 1993), 141.

[16] Fee, *Gospel and Spirit*, 7-8.

[17] Ibid., 8.

[18] John F. MacArthur, *Charismatic Chaos* (Grand Rapids, MI: Zondervan, 1992), 231.

[19] Ibid.

[20] Deere, 54-55.

should be. Since one who speaks in tongues speaks in a language that neither he nor his hearers understands, the companion gift of the interpretation of tongues is necessary to make the utterance intelligible.

One popular opinion in Pentecostal and Charismatic circles is that an utterance in tongues is a word *from* God. In fact utterances in tongues are commonly referred to as messages in tongues.[21] This indicates that God is speaking to His people via the gift of tongues and interpretation. This understanding of the gifts is widespread. It can be found in scholarly works such as commentaries.[22] It can also be found in books that are written on a more popular level.[23] This view is expressed in the writing of classical Pentecostal, Donald Gee.[24] Even those who would not be considered classical Pentecostals hold this view.[25] This view is, essentially, tongues plus interpretation equals prophecy.[26] This belief informs the contemporary use of tongues and interpretation. Many, if not most, of the modern-day expressions of these gifts are messages from God.

The scriptural foundations of this belief can be found in First Corinthians 14. In First Corinthians 14:6, the apostle Paul raises a question about what benefit he would be to the Corinthians if he came to them speaking in tongues. He implies that he would be of no benefit to them unless he brought them a revelation, prophecy, or a word of instruction. One commentator sees in this text the possibility of tongues with the accompanying gift of interpret-

---

[21] Gordon D. Fee, *God's Empowering Presence: The Holy Spirit in the Letters of Paul* (Peabody, MA: Hendrickson Publishers, 1994), 218.

[22] C. K. Barrett, *The First Epistle to Corinthians* (New York: Harper & Row, 1968; reprint, Peabody, MA: Hendrickson Publishers, 1987), 319 (page citations are from the reprint edition).

[23] Dennis Bennett and Rita Bennett, *The Holy Spirit and You: A Study-Guide to the Spirit-Filled Life* (Plainfield, NJ: Logos International, 1971), 85.

[24] Donald Gee, *Concerning Spiritual Gifts*, rev. ed. (Springfield, MO: Gospel Publishing House, 1972), 63-64.

[25] C. Peter Wagner, *Your Spiritual Gifts Can Help Your Church Grow* (Glendale, CA: Regal Books, G/L Publications, 1979), 233.

[26] Barrett, 316.

ation being one of these things.[27] The other text used to support the view that tongues are a word from the Lord is First Corinthians 14:21. This verse, which is adapted from the Old Testament, refers to God speaking to people through strange tongues. Pentecostal writer, Donald Gee, sees in this text support for the idea of tongues being a message from God.[28]

Another view regarding the gift of tongues sees it as a word *to* God. In this view, the direction of the communication is reversed; God's people are speaking to Him. Of the two views regarding the contents of an utterance in tongues, this is certainly less widely known and practiced. One advocate of this view is Gordon Fee.[29] Another scholar who leans strongly in this direction is Craig Keener.[30] Some of the previously cited authors such as the Bennetts and Donald Gee also accept this expression of the gift.

The understanding of the gift as communication from the believer to God sees tongues primarily as praise and worship. This seems to be a common understanding of the private use of tongues but not of the public gift with interpretation. While the view that the gift of tongues is a word to God may be the minority view, at least in practice, it has strong biblical foundations.

The scriptural support of this view is found in Paul's direct statement in First Corinthians 14:2 that the one who speaks in a tongue does not speak to men but to God. Also in favor of this understanding of the gift are the words that Paul uses to describe the gift of tongues. Paul describes tongues as prayer, praise, and thanksgiving (1 Cor. 14:14, 16-17).[31] All of these words describe activities that are properly directed to God.

The gift of tongues, along with the gift of interpretation, provides a supernatural connection between God and His people in which communication

---

[27] Ibid, 317.

[28] Gee, 63,63.

[29] Fee, *God's Empowering Presence*, 217, 223.

[30] Craig S. Keener, *3 Crucial Questions About the Holy Spirit*, 3 Crucial Questions Series (Grand Rapids, MI: Baker Books, 1996), 121.

[31] Craig S. Keener, *Gift & Giver: The Holy Spirit for Today* (Grand Rapids, MI: Baker Academic, 2001), 123.

takes place. These gifts when properly exercised serve to greatly bless God's people.

This now brings us to the consequences of the gift, that is, the effect or impact that the gift has when it is in operation. There are some in the church who do not like the word *experience*. To them, it is a term that stands in tension with the authority of Scripture. While experiences should never be exalted above Scripture, this does not mean that all experience should be shunned. Scripture and experience are not mutually exclusive. Part of the purpose of Scripture is to lead us into an experience with God. If God is still the living God (1 Tim. 3:15), it should be expected that His people will exper- ience Him as the New Testament church did.

The gift of tongues as described in First Corinthians 14 is for congrega- tional use and the common good (1 Cor. 12:7). When tongues are expressed in a church meeting, they come through an individual who is the first to experience them. This individual serves as the human vessel through whom God graces the meeting. Whether they are conscious of it or not, this person experiences a number of important things.

First, the individual experiences the presence of the Lord. While it is true that God is everywhere present, this is a manifest presence. God is not only with the individual but moving through him or her by His Spirit.

Another thing that the individual experiences in exercising the gift of tongues is being chosen. He or she has been prompted to speak by the Spirit. Of all of the assembled worshipers, the Lord has called upon this individual to minister to the church as a whole through this public gift. This should be both a holy and a humbling experience since it is the Holy Spirit who distrib- utes the gifts (1 Cor. 12:11).

A third thing that the individual experiences is the grace aspect of the gifts. This is particularly evident in the gift of tongues. The speaker is not speaking a known language by natural ability but is speaking an unknown language by supernatural ability. He is doing something that he could not do on his own. So there is a blessing for the individual Christian whom God uses to exercise the public gift of tongues.

The gift, once manifested through the individual, brings about a corporate experience of the gift. The other worshipers are now aware that something is happening in the assembly, and this has an effect on them.

The first effect tongues produces in the congregation is the same that it produced for the individual, namely an awareness of the presence of the Lord. God is in their midst and is making that clear through the manifestation of the gift. This generally results in a hush falling upon the congregation as the speaker, inspired by the Holy Spirit, utters words in an unknown tongue. This is a holy moment and is usually one that is characterized by a great awe and reverence for God.

The public gift of tongues also produces a sense of anticipation. For the gift is not complete without the companion gift of the interpretation of tongues (1 Cor. 14:5,13, 27-28). The worshipers now wait to hear, in their own language, what has been previously said in a language that they did not know. Those who have been in services where these gifts have been in operation know the effect that they can have upon the congregation. It can be a very rich experience.

But experience without purpose means nothing. God gives the gifts of the Spirit, including tongues, for a purpose. The divine intention is declared to be edification (1 Cor. 14:4-5). The edification provided by the gift is both individual and corporate. The apostle Paul states very clearly that the person who speaks in tongues edifies himself (1 Cor. 14:4); he is somehow built up in his faith by speaking in tongues. Some may question how this can be since the individual does not know what he is saying. While speaking in tongues does not appeal to the logical or analytical mind, it is of benefit. There are at least two reasons why it is of benefit.

The first has to do with the source of the gift. God is the giver of the gift, and God gives good gifts (Jas.1:17). Since God knows all things, including what will benefit us, we should believe that these unintelligible tongues serve a purpose. They contribute to the edification of the individual believer.

In other words, they fulfill the divine intention for which they were given.

The second reason why they edify the believer is because of what they are. Paul describes tongues as prayer, praise, and thanksgiving (1 Cor. 14:14-16). These are all parts of communication with God. Anything that increases or strengthens our communication with God will build us up in our faith.

The gift of tongues can provide edification to the congregation if the tongues are interpreted (1 Cor. 14:5). The tongues, once interpreted, are understood by the congregation and can serve to edify them in one of two ways.

First, they can be a source of great encouragement as God speaks to His people and gives them direction and comfort. Thus, tongues and interpretation function as prophecy (1 Cor.14:5). This contemporary word from the Lord can be a great help to the people of God as they are reminded that He knows where they are and that He cares for them. They may also be touched by the fact that they have been granted time in heaven. God took the time to speak to them.

The second way in which tongues can edify the congregation is in the area of worship. If the interpreted utterance is prayer and praise, this inspired worship can enhance the worship of the entire congregation. As the praise is offered, the people become aware of the greatness of God and in greater numbers and intensity enter into worship. This manifestation of the gift serves to make worship contagious.

In this article, we have seen that the gift of tongues is a controversial gift. While definitely present in the first-century church, its presence in the contemporary church is sometimes questioned. We have also seen that the cessationist's position rests on strained scriptural interpretation, the history of the post-apostolic church, and his or her own experience.[32] Cessationists lack a clear word from the Lord that the gift of tongues has passed from the church. We have also seen the purposes that the gift served in the early church and the great benefits that it provided both to the individual who

---

[32] Deere, 55-56.

exercised the gift and to the congregation. These things cannot be minimized. God gave the gift of tongues to the church to strengthen it (1 Cor.14:26).

The outpouring of the Spirit is a characteristic of the last days.[33] The last days began in the first century A.D., the time of the apostolic church, and will continue until the Lord's return.[34] In view of this fact, we should expect the presence of spiritual gifts in the church today. The church is still in need of the edification and strengthening that the gifts provide.[35] Since this is so, we dare not exclude any of the spiritual gifts from the church.

---

[33] Oss, 266-267.

[34] Ibid.

[35] Deere, 135.

Chapter 2   Desire Prophecy

The subject of spiritual gifts is one of the on-going controversies in the contemporary church. Sincere, Bible-believing Christians are divided over this very important issue. Some in the church maintain that certain gifts of the Spirit, such as tongues and prophecy, are not for today, while others, Charismatics and Pentecostals, maintain that all of the gifts exist, but in many cases, they emphasize speaking in tongues. Paul, who wrote the most extensively about spiritual gifts in the New Testament, would not endorse either of these views. In First Corinthians 14:1-12, the apostle Paul offers some counsel that serves as a corrective to both of these positions. Participants on both sides of the debate would do well to read and heed Paul's words in this passage. In this text Paul commends the gift of prophecy to the Corinthian believers. In the remainder of this article, we will examine the passage, giving particular attention to the gift of prophecy in order to learn what Paul thinks are the most important issues concerning spiritual gifts. In considering Paul's words, we will note the character of the gifts of tongues and prophecy and the historical context to which Paul addressed himself in First Corinthians.

There is no question that the gift of prophecy existed in the New Testament church. References to prophets and prophecy are found in a number of places in Paul's writings and in the Book of Acts. Gordon Fee says that of all of the spiritual gifts, Paul mentions prophecy in his letters more than any of the other gifts.[36] But what was this gift? Drawing on the biblical record in First Corinthians 14, Fee defines prophecy as "spontaneous, Spirit-inspired,

---

[36] Gordon D. Fee, *Paul, the Spirit, and the People of God* (Peabody, MA: Hendrickson, 1996), 170.

intelligible messages, orally delivered in the gathered assembly, intended for the edification or encouragement of the people."[37]

The Corinthian believers were no strangers to spiritual gifts. In First Corinthians 1:7, Paul says that they "do not lack any spiritual gift." They were charismatic, and they knew what prophecy was. This is evident not only from the mention of the gift in chapters 12 and 13 and the instructions regarding its use in chapter 14 but also from the instructions that he gives concerning women prophesying in chapter 11. Since the church seemingly had a wealth of spiritual gifts, why did Paul single prophecy out and give the teaching that we find in First Corinthians 14:1-12?

One possible reason for Paul's instruction was that the Corinthians' understanding of the gift of prophecy may have been colored by the pagan exercise of prophecy, most notably at Delphi.[38] New Testament scholar, Craig S. Keener, however, does not see cultural background as being especially important in reference to this issue.[39] So, the idea that Paul wrote as he did to counteract pagan ideas regarding prophecy is not entirely certain.

What is more certain is the condition of the Corinthian church. It was a divided church. Examples of division can be seen in the letter in relation to teachers, wisdom, legal matters, marriage, divorce, and idol feasts.[40] Their divisiveness also carried over into areas of worship, namely communion and spiritual gifts.[41] The Corinthians' intense individualism is in part due to their being a product of their culture. First-century Roman Corinth was marked by

---

[37] Gordon D. Fee, *God's Empowering Presence: The Holy Spirit in the Letters of Paul* (Peabody, MA: Hendrickson, 1994), 170.

[38] Ben Witherington III, *Conflict & Community in Corinth: A Socio-Rhetorical Commentary on 1 and 2 Corinthians* (Grand Rapids, MI: Wm. B. Eerdmans/Carlisle, Cumbria: Paternoster, 1995), 276-279.

[39] Craig S. Keener, *The IVP Bible Background Commentary: New Testament* (Downers Grove: InterVarsity, 1993), 480.

[40] Witherington, 241.

[41] Ibid, 247, 253.

boasting, self-promotion, and the desire for public recognition.[42] The Corinthians brought these characteristics into their new faith.[43] The "world" had invaded the church, and Paul was seeking to remedy the situation in many areas including spiritual gifts.

A third explanation for Paul's words in First Corinthians 14 is that he was writing to the church about spiritual gifts because they had previously written to him about them.[44] Let us now turn our attention to a more detailed consideration of Paul's teaching in First Corinthians 14:1-12.

Before focusing on the gift of prophecy, we need to note how Paul opens the passage. He begins in verse one by telling the Corinthian believers to "follow the way of love and eagerly desire spiritual gifts." Fee tells us that these instructions are imperatives.[45] Thus, they are not mere suggestions but orders. Morris tells us that the word *follow* means to "pursue with persist-ence."[46] In chapter 13 Paul had taught them extensively on the subject of love. By beginning chapter 14 with telling them to "follow the way of love," Paul is indicating that love has application to the subject of spiritual gifts. As someone has said, the gifts of the Spirit should be exercised by the fruit of the Spirit. From what Morris has told us about the word *follow*, this is to be done in an ongoing fashion. In view of what follows in chapter 14, Paul may have instructed the church to "desire spiritual gifts" so that they did not misun-derstand his instructions as a negative view of the gifts. And most certainly he urges them to desire spiritual gifts because they are good for the church.

---

[42] Ibid , 8.

[43] Ibid.

[44] Bruce W. Winter, *After Paul Left Corinth: The Influence of Secular Ethics and Social Change* (Grand Rapids, MI: Wm. B. Eerdmans, 2001), 1.

[45] Gordon D. Fee, *The First Epistle to the Corinthians*, The New International Commentary on the New Testament (Grand Rapids, MI: Wm. B. Eerdmans, 1987), 653.

[46] Leon Morris, *The First Epistle of Paul to the Corinthians*, Tyndale New Testament Commentaries, reprint (Leicester, England: InterVarsity/Grand Rapids, MI: Wm. B. Eerdmans, 1983), 190.

First Corinthians 12:7 makes it clear that this is the purpose of the gifts. So, Paul's introductory remarks tell us that the gifts are to be sought, and they also tell us the "spirit" in which they are to be exercised.

In the last part of verse 1, Paul especially commends the gift of prophecy to his readers. Since the letter is addressed to the church as a whole, Witherington reminds us that any believer could be used in the gift of prophecy.[47] But why is there this emphasis on prophecy (seemingly over against tongues)? Barrett believes that it is because the Corinthians had an exaggerated view of the importance of tongues.[48] Morris also shares this view.[49] Paul does compare and contrast the two gifts, and he has an obvious preference for prophecy. Fee says that what Paul is taking issue with is not tongues, but tongues that are not interpreted.[50] Also in commenting on the passage, Fee says that "the concern is edification (v. 3-5), the issue intelligibility."[51] This is a very good assessment of the situation. With this in mind, let us now give our attention to what Paul says about the gifts of tongues and prophecy.

The two gifts have a couple of common characteristics in that they are both gifts of the Spirit and both verbal gifts, but there are significant differences between them as well. In verse 2, Paul gives us some details about the gift of tongues. He tells us that those who speak in tongues direct their speech to God, not to men. Part of the reason for this is that no one understands them because they are speaking mysteries and not the native language of the congregation. By way of contrast, in verse 3, Paul describes the gift of prophecy. One who is prophesying speaks to men (note the direction of the speech) for their strengthening, encouragement, and comfort (note also the contents of the prophetic message). In order for people to receive the benefits of this communication, they must be able to understand it. Prophecy,

[47] Witherington, 281.
[48] C.K. Barrett, *The First Epistle to the Corinthians* (New York: Harper & Row, 1968; reprint, Peabody, MA: Hendrickson, 1987), 315.
[49] Morris, 190.
[50] Fee, *Corinthians*, 653.
[51] Ibid.

then, is spoken in the native language of the congregation. Thus, the issue of intelligibility can be clearly seen here.

A further contrast between the two gifts is drawn in verse 4. This contrast has to do with the benefits that the gifts produce. The person who speaks in tongues edifies (or builds himself up), whereas the person who prophesies edifies or builds up the church.

In this contrast the issue of edification comes into view. Edification of the church body as a whole only takes place when those gathered understand what is being said. This accounts for Paul's preference for the gift of prophecy. Prophecy is intelligible. Paul wants more people to be served. If the church continues to give excessive attention to uninterpreted tongues, the church will remain individualistic, as each one will be concentrating only on building himself up. This, in the long run, will be detrimental to the life of the church and is, in fact, contrary to the purpose for which God gave spiritual gifts; God gave them for the common good (1 Cor.12:7).

Now, this is not to say that the gift of tongues is an undesirable gift. It is a gift that has come from God (1 Cor.12:10) and as such has its place. Later in the chapter, Paul says that he speaks in tongues (14:18). He further shows the desirability of tongues in First Corinthians 14:5 when he says that he would like every one of them to speak in tongues. So, Paul is not against speaking in tongues, but he would rather have the Corinthians prophesy when gathered together as a church. The latter part of verse 5 makes it clear that this is because he wants the church (as a whole) to be edified.

In verse 5 Paul also states, in a qualified sense, the superiority of prophecy over tongues. The qualification can be seen in Paul's statement that "he who prophesies is greater than one who speaks in tongues *unless he interprets...*" (emphasis mine). Here again, as the latter part of the verse makes clear, the issue is intelligibility. This verse has led some commentators to conclude that tongues plus interpretation equals prophecy; C. K. Barrett holds this position.[52] Leon Morris also seems to subscribe to this view,

---

[52] Barrett, 316.

claiming that man receives a message from the gift of tongues when it is accompanied by interpretation.[53] Though, in practice, many utterances in tongues are interpreted as a message *from* God, biblically speaking, it seems that tongues ought to be worship, or a message *to* God. I am indebted to charismatic scholar Craig S. Keener for pointing out that tongues is prayer (which would be directed to God).[54] Gordon Fee also holds this view.[55] Spirit-inspired worship can be a great blessing.

In verse 6, Paul raises the question of what benefit he would be to the Corinthians if he came to them speaking in tongues. He implies that he would be of no value to them unless he brought them something intelligible (revelation, knowledge, prophecy, or word of instruction). He then goes on to show the importance of intelligibility. In verses 7 and 8 he uses two examples involving musical instruments to make his point. The first one involves a flute or harp. Ferguson says that the word should be pipe, not flute.[56] Be that as it may, Paul's point is not lost. If the notes are not clearly sounded, no one will recognize the song that is being played. In the same way, in a battle situation one will not know what instructions are being given if the notes of the trumpet call cannot be discerned. In order for any benefit to be received, one must understand. That the instrument examples relate to Paul's argument about spiritual gifts is borne out by verse 9 where he says, "So it is with you," and then proceeds to speak about tongues. Paul's point: they must speak intelligibly in order to benefit each other. In verses 10 and 11, Paul acknowledges that there are many languages in the world and that they all have meaning, but if their meaning cannot be grasped, then the words spoken are of little value to the hearer. In verse 12, Paul again states that the Corinthians should channel their zeal for spiritual gifts toward those gifts

---

[53] Morris, 192.

[54] Craig S. Keener, *3 Crucial Questions About the Holy Spirit*, 3 Crucial Questions Series (Grand Rapids, MI: Baker, 1996), 121.

[55] Fee, *Corinthians*, 659.

[56] Everett Ferguson, *Backgrounds of Early Christianity*, 2nd edition (Grand Rapids, MI: Wm. B. Eerdmans, 1993), 98.

that will benefit the church as a whole. Morris states it well: "The great thing for the Christian is that he may be able to edify others."[57] That is the point that Paul is trying to make to the divided Corinthian church.

Paul's message in this text has great contemporary relevance. To members of the body of Christ, who deny or downplay the gifts of the Spirit, Paul says to desire or seek them. To other believers, who have and exercise the gifts, Paul would say, make sure that you exercise them in the proper spirit, which is love, and for the proper purpose, the edification of the church. There is no room for spiritual pride or showmanship in the church; we are empowered to serve. To those in the Pentecostal or Charismatic churches who are in some sense duplicating the Corinthian error of overemphasis on tongues, Paul would say that there are other gifts as well that can edify the church and they should be sought because the church needs all of them. Finally, Paul's words tell us that we have a God who desires to communicate with us and build us up in the faith. He desires to do this, at least in part, by speaking through various members of the body. May we be great seekers of His gifts, good stewards of His grace (1 Pet. 4:10), and grateful recipients of His servants for the upbuilding of His church.

---

[57] Morris,194.

Chapter 3   The Spirit: Working to What End?

The Holy Spirit is an important person in biblical history. The fact that He is God, the third Person of the Trinity, is enough to substantiate that truth, but the many references to Him in the New Testament underscore His importance. The Holy Spirit fills a vital role in the plan of God. Though unseen by the human eye, His influence can often be seen and felt. In this article, we will survey Luke's references to the Holy Spirit in his gospel, and note, in context, what he says about the activity of the Spirit. We shall also make brief mention, in the course of this article, of the theme of the Spirit in some of the texts in the Book of Acts. These references are not random; the Spirit is at work in the overall purposes of God. After surveying these references to the Spirit, we shall attempt to show the thread that links them all together.

Most of Luke's explicit references to the Spirit occur in the first four chapters of his gospel. The first reference is in 1:15 and refers to the fact that John the Baptist will be filled with the Holy Spirit before he is born. This fact helps to explain what is said about him later in verses 16 and 17: "Many of the people of Israel will he bring back to the Lord their God. And he will go on before the Lord, in the spirit and power of Elijah, to turn the hearts of the fathers to their children and the disobedient to the wisdom of the righteous—to make ready a people prepared for the Lord." In short, the Spirit is the One who will equip him to be effective in the work that the Lord has called him to.

The second reference to the Spirit is also found in chapter 1 and concerns the moving of the Spirit upon the Virgin Mary concerning a child (1:35). The child in view this time is Jesus Christ. The angel, Gabriel, has told Mary that she is going to have a baby; since she is a virgin, she asks how this can be. Gabriel replies that the Holy Spirit will come upon her and enable her to conceive this child. So, in this text, the Holy Spirit is providing supernatural empowerment so that a woman, without the aid of a human father, could conceive and have a child. God is overriding human impossibilities. This is the means whereby Jesus, the Savior, will be both fully God and fully man.

After Mary's encounter with the angel, Gabriel, we find another reference to the activity of the Holy Spirit. This time the Spirit is moving upon another woman, Elizabeth, who would be the mother of John the Baptist (1:41). When Mary, her cousin, comes to visit her and greets her, the baby in Elizabeth's womb leaps; Elizabeth is filled with the Holy Spirit and begins to prophesy. In this passage, we see that the Holy Spirit gives Elizabeth supernatural revelation about things that she would not know naturally. At this point, Mary was probably not visibly pregnant, and yet Elizabeth knows that Mary is carrying a child. She also knows that Mary, unlike Zechariah, believed the message that she had received from the angel. Most importantly, she knows the identity of the child that Mary carries. He is the Lord.

Elizabeth's husband, Zechariah, is the next person on whom we see the Spirit move (1:67). He had been unable to speak because he did not believe the message of the angel that he was going to have a son. At the baby's circumcision, when asked what the name of the baby was to be, he wrote— John. After that, he was able to speak, and he began to prophesy: he praised the Lord; spoke about the ministry of his son, John the Baptist; and recounted the faithfulness of the Lord to the patriarchs and to Israel in raising up a deliverer. Under the inspiration of the Spirit, Zechariah links the past and present workings of God.

The next reference to the Spirit is found in chapter two. In this chapter we see the Holy Spirit active in the life of an elderly saint by the name of Simeon. In fact, the activity of the Spirit is mentioned in three consecutive verses in reference to him (2:25-27). The first thing that we learn is that the Holy Spirit had revealed to Simeon that he would not die until he saw the

Lord's Christ (2:25-26). So, supernatural knowledge was given to him. The second thing that we see is that the Holy Spirit was active in Simeon's life, actually moving or directing him (geographically). As a result of the Spirit's work, he was led to the very place in the Temple where the Lord's Christ was, so that he could see Him. Once he saw the child, he took Him in his arms, and he knew immediately who the child was. This recognition must also have been a revelation of the Holy Spirit.

The next explicit reference to the ministry of the Holy Spirit is found in the third chapter (3:16). In this chapter, John speaks prophetically of an unnamed coming one. This coming one is Jesus Christ. At this time Jesus is an adult, and in this chapter we learn that Jesus is the one who will baptize with the Holy Spirit. Part of His ministry will be to dispense the Spirit upon His people (see also Acts 2:4,33).

A few verses later we find that the Holy Spirit comes upon Jesus Christ in bodily form right after John baptizes Him in water (3:22). This took place just prior to His embarking upon His public ministry (see 3:23). So this coming of the Spirit was to empower Him for the work that He was about to commence. The first verse of chapter 4 tells us that when Jesus came from the Jordan (where He was baptized), He was full of the Spirit. He was under the complete control of the Spirit. We find further that He, like Simeon mentioned above, was directed geographically; He was led by the Spirit into the wilderness to be tempted by the devil. We further find that though His time in the wildness was one of temptation and adversity, it did not have an adverse effect on His spiritual state, since He returned from the wilderness temptation in the power of the Spirit (4:14). Following closely on the heels of this text, we find Jesus in the synagogue of Nazareth reading from Isaiah 61 ("The Spirit of the Lord is on me"). He applies this verse (a Messianic prophecy) to Himself and tells the congregation that this Scripture is fulfilled. He is the anointed one spoken of in the Old Testament, and He is anointed for a purpose: to preach good news to the poor, to proclaim freedom to the prisoners, the recovery of sight to the blind, to release the oppressed, and to proclaim the year of the Lord's favor (4:18-19).

In chapter 10 we find a reference to the Holy Spirit in connection with Jesus (10:21). In this text Jesus is said to have been full of joy through the Holy Spirit. This took place right after Jesus told the seventy-two that they should not rejoice that the demons are subject to them; rather, they should rejoice in the fact that their names are written in heaven. Jesus had joy because of the work of God in and through His disciples' lives.

In the next chapter we find that the Holy Spirit is a good gift that is given by God the Father to those who ask Him (11:13). This verse informs us of something that we need to know, namely, that we do not earn or merit the Spirit's presence or activity in our lives. He is a gift given by our gracious God.

Chapter 12 contains the last explicit reference to the Holy Spirit. In this text we learn two things about the Spirit: first, that He can be sinned against (12:10); this particular sin is especially serious. In context, the sin is blasphemy against the Holy Spirit, and the one who commits it will not be forgiven. The second thing that we learn in this chapter is that the Holy Spirit is a teacher (12:12). In times of trial, when called upon to testify, the Holy Spirit will help the people of God. He will teach them what to say in their time of need; He will inspire them.

This concludes our consideration of the explicit references to the activity of the Holy Spirit in the gospel of Luke. There are other indirect references or allusions to the Holy Spirit's working, but I have not said anything about them because the Spirit was not explicitly mentioned. Examples of indirect references to the Holy Spirit included Luke 5:17 and 24:49.

The verses that I have cited in this article in reference to the Holy Spirit are quite varied. They involved different people, at different times, in different contexts, and have to do with different aspects of the Spirit's work. Nonetheless, there is a common thread that ties them all together: salvation history. At each juncture, the Holy Spirit is witnessing to or moving things forward regarding the salvation that is to be found in Jesus.

In Luke 1:15, John the Baptist was filled with the Holy Spirit in his mother's womb so that he could be effective in being the forerunner for the Messiah, Jesus Christ. In 1:35, the Holy Spirit was instrumental in physically producing the body of Jesus in Mary's womb, so that the incarnation could take place. In 1:41, as Elizabeth prophesies under the anointing of the Spirit, she becomes aware of the identity of the child that Mary carries. Her words might also serve as a confirmation to Mary of the things that were spoken to her by Gabriel. Zechariah's prophecy (1:67) announces the role that his son will play in God's plan and also announces that God has raised up salvation in the house of David in faithfulness to what He had said in the past. Simeon's experience in the Temple also focused on the topic of salvation. The Spirit had revealed to him that he would see the Lord's Christ before he died, and the Spirit actually led, or directed, him to see the child Jesus in the Temple when Mary and Joseph brought Him there to be circumcised. His words over Jesus also spoke of salvation (2:30).

The next grouping of texts has to do with Jesus and the Spirit. In 3:16, we read that Jesus is the one who baptizes with the Holy Spirit. This will have significance later in the Book of Acts for Jesus' followers in reference to carrying the message of salvation to the world. In Luke 3:22, we find that Jesus was anointed by the Spirit prior to beginning His public ministry (3:23), which was a mission of salvation. All of the references in in the fourth chapter (4:1,14,18) have to do with the equipping and direction of the Messiah as He engages in the mission of salvation. The text in 10:21 shows the rejoicing of the Lord over the saving work that the Father has done in the lives of people. Luke 11:13 tells us that God gives the Holy Spirit to those who ask Him; evidence of this will be seen in the Book of Acts. In Luke 12:10, the sin of blasphemy against the Holy Spirit is mentioned. This sin is speaking against the Holy Spirit who has anointed Jesus for His Messianic mission (see Luke 4:18-19). The last direct reference to the Holy Spirit is found in Luke 12:12. In this verse we learn that the Holy Spirit teaches Jesus' followers what they are to say when they are "called on the carpet." This seems to be a situation in which testimony for the Lord would be given.

The importance of the Holy Spirit in the advance of the gospel extends beyond the ministry of Jesus to His disciples as well. In Acts 1:8, His disciples are promised power to be witnesses to Him in the world after the Holy Spirit comes upon them. In Acts 2:4, we find that they receive the promise and Peter preaches with the result that 3,000 are saved. The importance of the Spirit for gospel ministry is seen in other places in Acts as well (Acts 4:8, 31; 7:55; 9:17). So the Spirit is intricately tied to the mission of salvation: its inception, revelation, and advance from biblical times right on through to the end of the age. May God help us to carry on our mission in the fullness of the Spirit.

Chapter 4   The Spirit and the Word

The Holy Spirit is a very important person; He is God, the third person of the Trinity. This is a truth found in the Scriptures and affirmed in church creed; it is the official and historic position of the church and is readily accepted by evangelical Christians. The Bible, especially the New Testament, contains many references to the work that the Holy Spirit carries out. He is one who convicts of sin (John 16:8); indwells the believer (Rom. 8:9; Eph. 1:13); sanctifies (Rom. 8:13; Gal. 5:17ff); teaches (John 14:26); empowers (Acts 1:8); and gives spiritual gifts (1 Cor. 12:11). Theologically, we understand the kinds of things that He does, but on a practical level, identifying His work is not always easy. Being a spirit, He is invisible (though He can, on rare occasion, take on a tangible form as He did at the baptism of Jesus where He assumed the form of a dove). Thus, the only way that we can perceive His work is to look for certain results in keeping with the work ascribed to Him in the Scriptures. Some of His work is very visible and readily observable. For example, if a Christian prays for a sick person and that person is instantly healed, the spiritual gift of healing, which is given by the Holy Spirit, is very likely in operation. In the same way, if someone exercises the gift of tongues in a public meeting, we can readily recognize the presence of the Spirit. However, some of the other activities of the Spirit are less observable. For example, the work of the Holy Spirit in sanctification is not usually as easily seen. While it is true that we are sanctified or made holy when we become believers in Jesus, there is also the practical daily sanctification in the life of the believer. This sanctification is a process in which the Lord is making us holy; we become aware of this over a period of time. There is one area where the activity of the Spirit can be present but is not easily noticed. I am speaking of the activity of the Spirit in the preached Word. In what follows I hope to show that the Holy Spirit is very active in the preaching of the Word and that this truth can be substantiated from Scripture and from contemporary experience.

At a fundamental level, the Spirit is vitally connected to the Word of God. The Holy Spirit is the divine author of the Word (Acts 4:25; 2 Tim. 3:16; 2 Pet. 1:21). The Spirit's connection with the Word can also be seen in Ephesians 6 where we are told that the Word of God is "the sword of the Spirit"; the Spirit and the Word work together.[58] The Holy Spirit also grants assistance to those who preach the word (Act 4:8,31; 1 Cor. 2:4-5; 1 Thess. 1:5; 1 Pet. 1:12). When the Spirit and the Word connect, there can be powerful results; this is evident in the Book of Acts. On the first Christian Pentecost, after having received the baptism with the Holy Spirit, Peter stood up and preached in the city of Jerusalem and three thousand people were saved. The Scripture records that, upon hearing Peter's words, they were "cut to the heart" (Acts 2:37). The dramatic results indicate that the Spirit was responsible for making the preached Word effective. The early Pentecostal writer, Donald Gee, believed that the gift of the word of knowledge was exercised in the sermon. [59] This could be overlooked by many because it would not be set off by the words, "thus says the Lord," or some other similar phrase. In more contemporary times, Dr. R.T. Kendall says in the vision statement on his website, "The Word and the Spirit must come together; the result will be power.[60] His vision statement also says, "Expository preaching is vital to all ministry of the Holy Spirit.[61]

Though I have not seen the mass conversions that Peter witnessed when

---

[58] Graeme Goldsworthy, *Prayer and the Knowledge of God* (Leicester, England: Inter-Varsity Press, 2003), 81.

[59] Donald Gee, *Spiritual Gifts in the Work of the Ministry Today* (Springfield, MO: Gospel Publishing House, 1963), 24.

[60] R.T. Kendall, R.T. Kendall Ministries' Vision Statement. Online http://www.rtkendallministries.com (accessed May 2009).

[61] Ibid.

he spoke on the first Christian Pentecost, I can testify that God does bless the preached Word. I have witnessed this take place on occasion when I have preached. In the process of preaching, I have seen people exchange glances at one another or offer a gentle, friendly nudge to the person next to them. In these instances, they were responding to what was being said. But the Spirit has been at work at other times without there being such visible evidence. I only became aware of these instances as people in the congregation shared information with me at a later time.

One of these instances occurred a number of years ago when I was preaching through the Book of Acts. The text I was preaching on was Acts 15:36-41. This is the passage that deals with Paul and Barnabas parting company due to a disagreement about John Mark. On the week that I preached this text we had two people visit our church. As I explained the passage, I said that while God used the two groups of missionaries that emerged from the split, I did not think that what happened was God's best because of the conflict between the Christian workers. It turns out that the couple, who visited on this particular Sunday, was having a problem with division in their church. My remarks pointedly addressed their circum-stances (though I did not know it at the time). One of the people who regu-larly attended our church, who knew the couple, had to tell them that I knew nothing about the situation in their church.

On another occasion the Spirit used the sermon to work with a young man in our Sunday morning worship service. The man had some problems in his life and had not been in church for quite some time. I do not face the congregation during much of the worship service, and so I was not aware of some of the things that were taking place before I stood up to preach. I was told about these things when the service was over. Earlier in the service, my wife had gone over to this young man to talk to him and asked him to go to the altar. She told him that she would go up with him. He did not want to go. She spoke to him about God's call. As I closed the message on that Sunday, I mentioned God's call five times. At the end of the service, this man came forward for prayer.

God is at work among His people. He frequently uses the preached Word, even when we are not aware of it. One reason this happens is that the message may not be expressly touching a circumstance in our life at the time. Another reason that the power of the preached Word is not recognized is because some people do not share what they know has taken place. I would not have known about either of these situations mentioned above if people had not shared with me. While we should take confidence that God is at work in the preached Word, even if we do not see immediate visible results, becoming aware that God has been at work can be a great blessing. Perhaps some need to give testimony to the church of what God has been dealing with them about through the preached Word, or some should encourage their pastors by letting them know that God has been using them though their preaching. The Spirit and the Word are a powerful combination, working together to change lives.

Chapter 5   Recovering Divine Guidance

Divine guidance. When we hear these words, we typically think of God guiding us with reference to a decision that we need to make. This is certainly one aspect of what divine guidance is, but that is not what I am going to deal with in this article. In this article, I will be speaking about God directing us to a very specific ministry. The Book of Acts contains a number of examples of this type of guidance. Let us take a brief look at some of them.

In Acts 8, we find the account of the ministry of Philip the evangelist (Acts 21:8). Philip was one of the seven men chosen by the church in Jerusalem to help with the distribution to the widows (Acts 6:5). When persecution of the church erupted after the stoning of Stephen, Philip fled to Samaria and began to preach Christ (Acts 8:5). He had a very profitable ministry there: crowds listened to him, people were saved, and there were many healings, miracles, and deliverances (Acts 8:6-8). While he was in Samaria, an angel of the Lord spoke to him and gave him directions to go to a specific road (Acts 8:26). As he obeyed this direction, he meet up with an Ethiopian eunuch (Acts 8:27). The Holy Spirit then instructed him to go near the eunuch's chariot. Once near the chariot he started a conversation with the man. The man then invited Philip into his chariot. As a result of this divine guidance, Philip led the man to faith in Jesus and baptized him (Acts 8:30-38).

In Acts 9, we read of a disciple by the name of Ananias. We don't know very much about this man. In Acts 22, as Paul is speaking, he says that Ananias was a devout observer of the law and was highly respected by the Jews in the city of Damascus (Acts 22:11-12). We do not know if this man had the ministry of an apostle, prophet, evangelist, pastor, teacher, or deacon. It is possible that he was not any one of them. All that we are told is that he was a disciple. What is significant, and commendable, about him is that he was one who could hear God when God spoke. We do not know if he was in a time of prayer when the Lord spoke to him as we are not given any details. We are simply told that the Lord spoke to him in a vision. Ananias was open to the supernatural. The divine guidance that he was given was quite amazing in that it contained detailed directions to go to a specific place to minister to a specific person. While many of us might be thrilled to have God speak to us with such clarity, Ananias, on this occasion, was not. He did not like the assignment that God gave him (and one can certainly understand why), but he did obey and went to minister to Saul of Tarsus as God had directed him to do. Because Ananias accepted the divine guidance and ministered to Saul, Saul was healed of his blindness and was filled with the Holy Spirit (Acts 9:17-18).

In Acts 10, we find the apostle Peter receiving divine guidance. The centurion, Cornelius, had an encounter with an angel who told him to send to the city of Joppa for Peter (Acts 10:5). Cornelius obeyed this directive and sent two of his servants and a soldier to Joppa to bring Peter back (Acts 10:7-8). As God was supernaturally working with Cornelius, we find that He was also dealing supernaturally with Peter. We are told that Peter fell into a trance (Acts 10:10) and that he had a vision (Acts 10:17,19). In this vision, God was dealing with Peter about prejudice so that Peter would be responsive to the messengers sent from Cornelius when they arrived. In fact, shortly after the vision, the Holy Spirit specifically told Peter he was to go with the three men who were looking for him and that He, the Spirit, had sent them (Acts 10:19-20). Peter obeyed the divine guidance that he had received, and it resulted in Cornelius, his friends, and his relatives coming to faith in Christ and being filled with the Holy Spirit.

In Acts 16, we find God giving divine guidance to the apostle Paul. In fact, in this chapter Paul receives a number of specific leadings, two negative and one positive. Paul is on a missionary journey with some of his companions. During the course of their journey, they attempt to go into the province of Asia, and the Holy Spirit keeps them from entering (Acts 16:6). They also tried to enter Bithynia, but the Spirit would not allow them to go there either. God was closing doors. I take great comfort in this passage because it seems to show that even the great apostle Paul operated at times by trial and error. After receiving two experiences of negative guidance, the Lord then supplied Paul with some positive guidance. We are told that Paul had a vision of a man of Macedonia asking him to come over and help them (Acts 16:9). The team discerned that this was where God wanted them to go. They obeyed the divine guidance, went to Macedonia, and it resulted in many people coming to faith in Christ in Philippi, Thessalonica, and Berea (Acts 16 and 17).

As we think about these texts, there are a number of things worth noting. First, the people who received divine guidance and ministered were both apostles and non-apostles. This tells us that one need not be a person in a position of spiritual leadership in order to be supernaturally directed by God. Second, in all of these cases there is no evidence that the people that God guided asked for this guidance. God took the initiative. The people simply heard God when He spoke, whether through an angel, vision, or by the Holy Spirit, and they responded to what He said. Third, in every case there was productive ministry that took place: people were blessed, some were saved, some were healed, and some were filled with the Holy Spirit.

The question that we need to ask ourselves is do we really expect this same kind of divine guidance today? Do we believe that God can direct us today by angels, visions, the prompting of the Spirit, dreams, and other means to just the right place at just the right time to minister to those in need? Theologically, we would probably answer "yes" to these questions. God is the living God (1 Tim. 3:15), and He is forever the same (Mal. 3:6; Heb. 13:8). But experientially, are we genuinely open to this kind of guidance? If we have consciously, or unconsciously, "written off" these types of divine guidance as things of the past or merely the thoughts of the spiritually unstable, let us repent. God has worked in these ways in the past, and He can do it again; therefore, let us listen for and anticipate such guidance as it produces very effective ministry.

Chapter 6   Spiritual Conceit

Spiritual conceit. It doesn't sound nice, and it isn't. It is, in reality, pride.
We might say that one who has it is "stuck on himself." The scary thing is
that we can sometimes be this person. The Bible tells us, "God opposes the
proud but gives grace to the humble" (Jas. 4:6). The Book of Proverbs warns
us of the dangers of pride (Prov. 11:2; 13:10; 16:18). Pride was an issue that
Jesus and the apostles John and Paul addressed in their teachings found in
the New Testament. The fact that it is addressed in both the Old and New
Testaments shows us that pride has been a long-standing problem for the
human race. All forms of pride are offensive, but spiritual conceit is one form
of pride that is particularly noxious.

In Luke 18, Jesus told a parable about a Pharisee and a tax collector. In the
parable, the two men were going to prayer. The Pharisee takes the opportunity to tell God how good he is. He offers God thanks that he is not like
other men; he also takes the opportunity to tell the Lord how much he does.
He is a very zealous religious person; he fasts and tithes. In his prayer, he
does not worship God or offer a request for a need, either for himself or
someone else, and his "thanks" leave much to be desired. His attention is
actually more on his neighbor than on God. By contrast, the tax collector
does not come to God with any sense of pride. He recognizes that he is a
sinner, and he merely comes to God and asks for mercy. The "surprise" of the
parable is that God accepts the tax collector's piety and rejects that of the
Pharisee. The Pharisee fell into a fatal trap in this parable: he compared
himself with someone else. This is a dangerous thing to do. If we look
around, we can always find someone who appears to be more sinful than we
are, but doing so does not make us any better. We are all going to be judged

by God's standard, not how we measure up against someone else. If we use a flawed form of measurement, we will arrive at a false conclusion. This faulty conclusion can give us a false sense of security as to our own standing before God. One of the hazards of this form of pride is that we are frequently not aware that we have it. Spiritual conceit can easily creep in undetected. In the parable, both of the men were engaged in the spiritual practice of prayer. During prayer, the Pharisee engaged in a kind of "spiritual one-upmanship." He had a spiritual superiority complex.

One area in which this can happen to us is in the area of spiritual experi-ence. As Pentecostals, we can sometimes speak as though our non-Pente-costal friends are somehow second-class citizens because they do not have the Baptism with the Holy Spirit. One need only read Paul's first letter to the Corinthians to see that Paul called a church that was very Pentecostal, "worldly" (1 Cor. 3:1). We need to be on guard against spiritual conceit: "I have something that you don't!" Even within our own ranks we can alienate one another; we can make those with the gift of helps feel less important than those who have the gift of healing. Paul took the Corinthians to task about this very issue. So spirituality can be an area in which we can fall into spiritual conceit.

Another area in which one can be become spiritually conceited is in the area of knowledge. Paul wrote, "knowledge puffs up" (1 Cor. 8:1). That is, knowledge can make someone proud; a person can get a "big head" because of what they know (or think they know). We see this also in the New Testa-ment. In John 7:49, the Jewish leaders of Jesus' day were angry with some temple guards because they did not arrest Jesus and bring Him in as they had been instructed. The guards said, "No one ever spoke the way this man does" (John 7:46). The Pharisees' reply to the guards (John 7:47-49) indicated that they felt that only those who had less biblical knowledge than they did believed in Jesus. The religious leaders thought that those who believed in Jesus were deceived. In truth, it was actually the other way around, and the Pharisees were supposed to be the religious experts! Their confidence in their own understanding of Scripture kept them from knowing the truth. Similar to those that Paul would later write about, they were "always learning but never able to come to acknowledge the truth" (2 Tim. 3:7). A number of times in the New Testament we find Jesus posing the question, "Have you never read?" to the religious leaders of the day (Matt.12:3,5; 19:4; 21:16,42; 22:31). They had certainly read these passages, but they did not understand them. Their learning had made them arrogant and unteachable. Knowledge of Scripture is important (2 Tim. 2:15), and we are to love God with our minds (Matt. 22:37), but we need to be careful about the spirit in which we hold this knowledge. Love and conceit are totally incompatible. We need to watch that we do not think more highly of ourselves than we ought (Rom. 12:3); this too is spiritual conceit.

In addition to spirituality and knowledge, there is yet another area in which spiritual conceit can rear its ugly head, and that is in the area of leadership. In his third epistle, the apostle John mentions a man by the name of Diotrephes. From what John writes, it seems that Diotrephes is a leader in the church. He has a lot of pull there, in fact, too much. He will not welcome traveling brethren who come to the church, and he stops those who want to welcome them; not content with that, he puts out of the church those who want to help the traveling ministers (3 John 10). John says that Diotrephes "loves to be first" (3 John 9). This man is a virtual dictator. His actions seem to indicate that he thinks that the church is his. He is in charge. He is abusive to those who he is supposed to serve. Pride of position is a potential problem for anyone in a leadership position whether the person is a pastor, Sunday School Superintendent, deacon, or trustee. Once one has a position or a title it can go to one's head. I remember when I first received my ministerial credentials. I really enjoyed the fact that now I was "Reverend." I am over that now, but it does not mean that I don't have to still be on my guard. Pride of position comes in many forms. This too is spiritual conceit. The biblical model of leadership is servanthood (Matt. 20:25). Lording it over people is forbidden (1 Pet. 5:3), whether it be though title or force of personality.

Spiritual conceit is a problem, but there is a solution for it. The first step is being aware that it exists and that it can enter our lives. If we don't think that is true, we had better go back and read what Paul said in his first epistle to the church in Corinth. In First Corinthians, Paul wrote, "If you think you are standing firm, be careful that you don't fall" (1 Cor. 10:12). Spiritual conceit is subtle, so we need to be watchful and alert. The corrective for all of this is to take seriously what the Scriptures teach; they speak constantly of the virtues of humility and servant leadership. These things are very basic and foundational, but they are things that we can easily drift away from. May God help us to guard our hearts (Prov. 4:23); if we seek to do this with God's help, He will keep us from falling prey to spiritual conceit.

Chapter 7   Women in the Pastoral Epistles

Addressing the subject of the place of women in society and the church from a biblical perspective is almost certain to get one into trouble, especially when the primary focus is the texts of the Pastoral Epistles. The non-Christian liberated women of the twenty-first century are largely uninterested in what the Bible has to say. They view scriptural teaching as archaic and restrictive; after all, they have "come a long way" and a few years ago were saying, "This is the '90s." They are predisposed to believe that to accept biblical teaching concerning women will certainly be a step backward. Even in the church there is not total agreement about the proper place of women. The divergent views that I refer to are not between liberal and conservative scholars, though those certainly exist, but between conservatives themselves. The place that Scripture assigns to women is a subject of great discussion and debate among those who revere the Bible as the Word of God. The various interpretations offered by scholars all use Paul's teachings to support their positions. Some intimate that the differences that exist are because there are some in the church who acknowledge the authority of Scripture and some who do not.[62] This is too simplistic an answer. There are reputable scholars to be found in the various schools of thought on this very controversial subject. As Fee and Stuart have indicated, the plain meaning of a text is not always so plain.[63] Discussing biblical teaching about women is a lot like discussing eschatology, as there are differences of opinion and emotions can run high.

---

[62] Homer A. Kent Jr., *The Pastoral Epistles*, rev. ed. (Chicago, IL: Moody Press, 1982), 110-111.

[63] Gordon D. Fee and Douglas Stuart, *How to Read The Bible for All It's Worth: A Guide to Understanding the Bible*, 2nd ed. (Grand Rapids, MI: Zondervan, 1993), 16.

All of this should not however cause us to shrink back from addressing this subject. God has addressed it, and we must apply ourselves to seeking to understand the Lord. The conclusions that we arrive at will color how we will interact with members of the female gender who are made in the image of God (Gen. 1:27).

In this article we shall consider what the apostle Paul teaches in the Pastoral Epistles concerning the place of women. Specifically, we shall look at the place of Christian women in culture and in the church. At appropriate points in this study, reference will be made to other Pauline texts to confirm, or draw out, Paul's teaching on this very important subject. Occasional references to the Book of Acts shall also be made. As the content of the Pastoral Epistles shows, some of the things that Paul wrote were intended as personal words or instructions for Timothy and Titus, and some of what he wrote was for the churches at large.[64] This being the case, all of the general instructions apply to men and women alike. Everyone in these Pauline churches was subject to the doctrinal and ethical directives that Paul sent to their particular congregations. In this article, we will not look at every text that refers to women. In this treatment of the Pastoral Epistles we are going to look only at texts that refer to a Christian woman's character and contributions in the context of the family and the community of faith. The relevant texts for this task are First Timothy 2:9-15; 3:11; 5:2ff; Second Timothy 1:5; 3:14-15; and Titus 2:3-5.

None of the above texts were written in a vacuum. They were addressed to real people, in real places, at a specific time. The two epistles bearing Timothy's name were sent to him and the church in Ephesus (1 Tim. 1:3), and the epistle addressed to Titus was for him and the church(es) on the island of Crete (Titus 1:5). Acceptance of the Pastoral Epistles as genuinely Pauline means that they are first-century documents written probably in the mid-sixties A.D.[65] Each of these epistles was sent to address a specific situation. They

---

[64] Kent, 20, 207.

[65] Craig S. Keener, *The IVP Bible Background Commentary: New Testament* (Downers

are, thus, occasional documents, "arising out of and intended for a specific occasion."[66] So, each of these writings is rooted in culture and history.

The first area that we will consider is the woman's place in culture. Christian women, like non-Christian women, of the first century pretty much had their place in life already determined for them. The culture was such that the primary sphere in which the woman was expected to function was the home or family. Her place in life was largely domestic. The family was the basic unit of society for all of the cultures in which early Christianity spread.[67] Thus, women, whether they were Christian or not, were expected to fill this family role. The place assigned to women in the Pastoral Epistles, in First Timothy 5:14 and Titus 3:3-5 in particular, is typical of the Greek perception of the family.[68] The ideal Greek wife was to be socially retiring, restricted mainly to the domestic sphere, quiet and obedient to her husband.[69] From these texts, it can be seen that the women's primary concerns were with responsibilities and relationships in the home with her husband and children. She was to be faithful and submissive to her husband (1 Tim. 5:9; Titus 2:5), and she was to have children (1 Tim. 5:14). These things are in keeping with what Paul teaches elsewhere in the New Testament (Rom. 7:2; Col. 3:18). While men may delight in Paul's words about wives submitting to their husbands, may we not forget Paul's words in Ephesians 5:21 that instruct all believers to submit to one another. Also, it should be noted that in one of the Pastoral passages, Paul gives the women some authority. In First Timothy 5:14, Paul says that the woman is to manage the home. She was to take care of the business of the home so that her husband could work. Her duties were probably similar to those placed upon the Jewish women of the day who

---

Grove, IL: InterVarsity Press, 1993), 607.

[66] Fee and Stuart, 48.

[67] Everett Ferguson, *Backgrounds of Early Christianity*, 2nd ed. (Grand Rapids, MI: Wm. B. Eerdmans Publishing Co, 1993), 65.

[68] Ibid, 70.

[69] Keener, *Background*, 638.

were expected to grind flour, do laundry, make beds, and spin wool.[70] This division of labor made it possible for a family to be adequately provided for. This is not to say that a woman should not, or could not, have a trade or profession under any circumstances (see Prov. 31; Acts 18:3). Thus, in the Pastoral Epistles, Paul is instructing the Christian women in Ephesus and on the island of Crete to fulfill the cultural expectations of wives and mothers in the first century. By doing this, they would help the cause of the gospel. In Titus in particular we see that Paul was very concerned about what outsiders or unbelievers thought of the behavior of Christians.[71] The behavior of Christians sends a message to the unbelieving world. What is conveyed can either draw people to Christ and the Christian message or drive them away. Paul, knowing that the message of the cross is an offense (1 Cor. 1:18-25), does not wish to put any unnecessary obstacles in people's way, so that they will be attracted to the Lord.

As was mentioned earlier, the woman's primary responsibility was to her husband and her children. The usual household tasks were listed as her responsibility. At this point, I would like to give attention to one particular aspect of the woman's responsibility toward the children. She was to teach them. This can be seen in a couple of places in the Pastoral Epistles. In First Timothy 5, which deals with the subject of widows, one of the qualifications for a widow that the church would provide for was that she had brought up children (5:10). The raising of children implies teaching. The mother, by virtue of her close association with the children, would be almost constantly teaching; both by her words and deeds the children would learn skills for life. They would learn from her how to eat, clean themselves, work around the home, and treat others respectfully. The teaching ministry of women can also be seen in a couple of other texts in the Pastoral Epistles. In Second Timothy 3:14-15, Paul tells Timothy that he is to continue in what he has

---

[70] Ferguson, 71.

[71] Gordon D. Fee, *1 and 2 Timothy, Titus*, NIBC (Peabody, MA: Hendrickson Publishers/Carlisle, Cumbria: Paternoster Press, 1995), 12.

learned because he (Timothy) knows from whom he learned these things. We know from the first chapter of the same epistle that the genuine faith that Timothy possessed his grandmother and mother also had before him (1:5). The implication of this text is that they instructed him in the faith. In addition, the mention in Second Timothy 3:15 that he knew the Scriptures from childhood also seems to confirm the fact that his mother and grandmother taught the Scriptures. Gordon Fee accepts the fact that they are among the ones from whom Timothy had learned the Scriptures.[72] That these women taught Timothy the Scriptures is probably the exception rather that the rule since most Jewish women were not well educated in the Law.[73] Nonetheless, Paul does not condemn what they had done. In Timothy's case, it was probably necessary, since his father was not a Jew and very likely did not have faith in the God of Scripture (Acts 16:1). Another type of teaching that Paul urges Christian women to participate in is that of the older women teaching the younger women (Titus 2:3-4). This teaching was to be done only by those Christian women who had character (Titus 2:3). The teaching enjoined here is not the teaching of Scripture (although the principles that they were to teach were in keeping with scriptural truth) but the practical instructions of how a woman should conduct herself in public and in private, in the home and in society. Specific areas of instruction to be covered in the teaching related to the woman's relationship with her husband and her children. The older women were to do the teaching presumably because they were experienced in these things and were people of integrity and respect. Both of these characteristics would make their teaching more believable and beneficial.

Now although the woman's primary sphere of activity in the first century was the family, this does not mean that family members were the only people that a woman had contact with. Her domestic responsibilities extended beyond those who lived in the home. She was responsible for those who came to the home. First Timothy 5:10 speaks of the godly widow, who may

---

[72] Fee, 278.

[73] Keener, *Background*, 611.

be enrolled by the church, as one who showed hospitality and washed the feet of the saints. Both of these qualifications have to do with her reception of guests and visitors who came to her home. Providing hospitality was giving suitable accommodations to travelers, who were strangers.[74] This provision would include both food and lodging. The washing of the saint's feet is reminiscent of the example of the Lord Jesus in John 13:3-8 and demonstrates servanthood.[75] The other two items in the list in First Timothy 5:10, namely, helping those in trouble and devoting herself to good deeds may have been carried out in the home or outside of it.

The societal, and now Pauline, ethics of the Pastoral Epistles were to be obeyed by the Christian women of Ephesus and Crete. But the obedience and servanthood that Paul enjoins was not to be merely a matter of outward show. It was to spring from an inner life that was disciplined and self-controlled. The fruit was to be an evidence of the root. Their self-control was to be seen in their speech (Titus 2:3) and in their appetites. In particular, they were to exercise self-control in their consumption of wine and in their sexuality (Titus 2:5).

Thus far we have seen the place that the Pastoral Epistles assign to women in the context of the family in first-century culture. We have noted the contributions and character that Paul says that women were to exemplify. There are some today who might not like some of the texts that we have looked at because they seem to say that "the woman's place is in the home." Those who object at this point probably do so because these texts don't seem to leave much space for a woman to have a job or a career outside of the home. The Bible does allow for this in other texts. Regardless of what one thinks of these passages in the pastorals we all have to come to terms with the fact that the home and family are important to God. Because this is so, we must also see the home and family as important and invest ourselves in them, as God desires. Serving in the home does not make one a second-rate

---

[74] Kent, 127-128.

[75] Keener, *Background*, 617.

citizen; neither is the home a prison from which one should seek to escape; this goes for men and women alike. Effective service in the home can produce healthy, happy, and holy relationships with God and others.

If the passages cited above have been a source of contention largely between the world and the church, the passages that we are about to discuss have been, indeed are, a source of contention within the church. The passages that I refer to are First Timothy 2:9-15 and First Timothy 3:11. These texts deal with the woman's place in the community of faith, the church. Women have been a part of the church from the earliest days (Acts 1:14; 2:1). Unlike the Gentiles, their membership in the church has never been questioned. Like men, they have been accepted by God through the blood of Christ and have become partakers of the Holy Spirit. The apostle Paul who penned the passages in the Pastoral Epistles that we will be looking at next also wrote, "There is neither Jew nor Greek, slave nor free, male nor female, for you are all one in Christ Jesus" (Gal. 3:28). He thus places both men and women on equal footing in Christ. But does this equality in Christ mean that women can do everything in the church that men can? Some in the church believe that women can be teachers and pastors up to and including senior pastor, and some do not. Still others take a more middle-of-the-road stance on this issue. The issue at hand is that of spiritual leadership. Can a woman hold a position of spiritual leadership in the church? The reason for the debate is largely due to Paul's words in First Timothy 2:11-12 where Paul enjoins silence and submission on the women and seemingly denies them the right to teach men or have authority over them. In reading the literature on the various sides of the debate, one can identify with the truth expressed in Proverbs 18:17: "The first to present his case seems right, till another comes forward and questions him." Those who oppose eldership for women appeal to Paul for their support, and those who are in favor of allowing women these positions also appeal to Paul for support. One scholar who holds to the traditional view, which would restrict women from positions where they could teach men, says that it is a question of biblical authority.[76] He is quite right. However, the implication is that if you do not accept his interpretation you do not acknowledge the authority of the Scriptures. Another scholar who holds to the egalitarian position, which would allow women to serve in these capacities, also affirms his belief in the Scripture's authority.[77] The issue ultimately comes down to what the Scriptures teach.[78] The problem of course is that not everyone agrees on what the Scriptures teach. So what are we to do?

Before looking at the passage which is at the center of the controversy regarding women's ministry (1 Tim. 2:9-15), let us look at another less-contested passage that has some bearing on the subject of women's ministry. This text is found in First Timothy 3:11: "In the same way, their wives are to be women worthy of respect, not malicious talkers but temperate and trustworthy in everything."

The individuals described in this verse are obviously female but there is a difference of opinion as to just who Paul is talking about in this verse. The two different options are that they are either the deacon's wives or deaconesses.[79] The difference between the two of course is that one is related to the minister by marriage and the other is the minister, the deacon. The NIV translation renders the word in the text, "wives." Gordon Fee admits that the Greek word could mean either "wife" or "woman."[80] C.K. Barrett also acknowledges that the Greek word is ambiguous.[81] So which interpretation is to be preferred and on what grounds?

Since the Greek word in the text is ambiguous, we have to look for help in

---

[76] Kent, 111.

[77] Craig S. Keener, *Paul, Women & Wives: Marriage and Women's Ministry in the Letters of Paul*, (Peabody, MA: Hendrickson Publishers, 1992), 11-12.

[78] Ibid, 3.

[79] Fee, 88.

[80] Ibid.

[81] C.K. Barrett, *The Pastoral Epistles*, New Clarendon Bible (London: Oxford University Press, 1963; reprint, Grand Rapids, MI: Outreach Publications, 1986), 61.

other places. We find that help in the context. Homer Kent gives us a couple of reasons for understanding this verse as a reference to women deacons. The first is that the third chapter of First Timothy deals with church leaders and their qualifications.[82] A second reason for understanding this verse as a reference to women deacons is that the Greek construction in the text indicates that another group (of leaders) is being introduced.[83] Also to be considered in this context is the question as to why there would be a list of qualifications for deacon's wives and not for overseers or bishop's wives if in fact the women in 3:11 were not deacons.[84] I find Kent's favoring of the deaconess interpretation interesting because he holds to the traditional (restrictive) school of thought regarding women elders.[85] While acknowledging that women can teach other women and the young, he does not feel that they should assume the position of authoritative teacher of Scripture in a context in which men are present.[86] Fortunately this is not the only text in the New Testament that deals with the subject of women deacons. The apostle Paul mentions one by name in his epistle to the Romans, Phoebe, a servant or deacon of the church at Cenchrea (Rom.16:1). So, it is reasonable to conclude that the New Testament church had women deacons.

The more controversial issue regarding women's ministry concerns the subject of eldership. Can a woman be an elder or an overseer? This is a subject of great debate within the church. The debate is fueled mainly by Paul's words in First Timothy 2:11-12, in which he enjoins silence and submission upon the women and forbids them to teach men. Let us therefore consider the two major schools of thought regarding the proper interpretation of this text.

The traditional view, which would prohibit a woman from teaching a

---

[82] Kent, 136.

[83] Ibid, 135.

[84] Don Williams, *The Apostle Paul & Women in the Church* (Glendale, CA: Regal Books, G/L Publications, 1977), 115.

[85] Kent, 108.

[86] Ibid.

man and thus also exclude her from eldership, holds that Paul's instructions in First Timothy 2:11-12 are applicable to the church in every place at every time. One reason for accepting this position is that the text does directly restrict the place of women. This viewpoint accepts the plain statement of the text. Another reason for seeing this text as binding on the church throughout the ages is that part of Paul's reason for writing First Timothy was so that Timothy would know how a church should be organized (1 Tim. 3:14-15).[87] Additional support for this view is found in the fact that the qualifications for eldership indicate that the individual should be a male (1 Tim. 3:1-2).[88] Also, there are no examples of women elders or bishops in the New Testament.[89] It is maintained that Paul explains his restriction of the teaching ministry of women on the basis of the creation order and the fall (1 Tim. 2:13-14).[90] The argument is that God created Adam first and so man takes preeminence in creation and that Eve took preeminence in the Fall (by being the first to sin); both of these facts relegate women to the place of submission.

The egalitarian view, which would permit women to teach men and be elders, holds that First Timothy 2:11-12 is the Word of God but that it must be understood in the particularity of the circumstances.[91] This view stresses the occasional nature of the text. The prohibition exists, but we can properly understand it (and apply it) only if we understand what was going on in Ephesus at the time.[92] The egalitarian position sees the prohibition as a temporary measure. In support of this position, it has been pointed out that verse 12, "I do not permit a woman to teach," would be better translated, "I am not permitting a woman to teach," implying that the restriction was due

---

[87] T. David Gordon, "A Certain Kind of Letter: The Genre of 1 Timothy," *Women in the Church: A Fresh Analysis of I Timothy 2:9-15*, eds. Andreas J. Kostenberger, Thomas R. Schreiner, and H. Scott Baldwin (Grand Rapids MI: Baker Books, 1995), 59-60.

[88] Kent, 121.

[89] Ibid.

[90] Ibid, 109.

[91] Keener, *Paul, Women*, 107.

[92] Ibid.

to a particular set of circumstances.[93] Additional evidence offered in support of the temporary nature of the restriction is that women were not educated in the Scriptures in those days.[94] This prompts Paul's radical directive (from a Jewish standpoint) that the women should learn.[95] Thus, one short-term remedy to help hinder the spread of error in Ephesus was to bar the women from teaching men; the long-term solution was to educate the women so that they could teach.[96] Also interesting is the fact that Paul has to tell Timothy that he is not permitting a woman to teach, as though this is something that Timothy does not know.[97] After working with Paul for as long as Timothy had, he certainly knew the standards and policies that Paul had for his churches, the stating of this directive seems to indicate that the directive was not a universal principle.[98]

Evidence outside of the Pastoral Epistles also calls into question the universality of the restriction in First Timothy 2:12. In Acts 18, we find Pricilla and Aquila teaching Apollos. This is the clearest example in the New Testament of a woman teaching a man. Then there are Euodia and Syntyche whom Paul says contended with him at his side in the cause of the gospel (Phil. 4:2-3). In addition, there are a number of women in Romans 16 that Paul speaks of as being in the ministry (see 16:1,3, 6-7,12). Now, unfortunately Paul does not give us the specifics of what the women did in ministry. I know that the argument from silence is not convincing or conclusive, but would it not make sense that at least some of these women, like Priscilla, were teaching the Word since laboring in the Lord includes spreading His Word? The arguments on both sides of the issue go on and on.

Let me try to bring this discussion to a close. There are no explicit examples of female elders in the New Testament; Priscilla in Acts 18 and

[93] Fee, 72.

[94] Keener, *Paul, Women*, 112.

[95] Keener, *Background*, 611.

[96] Keener, *Paul, Women*, 112.

[97] Ibid.

[98] Ibid.

Junias (Junia) of Romans 16 are as close as we get. But in view of Paul's references to women workers in the gospel, the fact that no other New Testament
epistle contains the prohibition of First Timothy 2:12, that the Greek construction in the text may indicate that the prohibition is temporary, and that
women now have the opportunity to be educated in the Scriptures, it would
seem that women should be permitted to hold places of leadership in the
church and engage in the preaching and teaching of the Scriptures to the
whole body of Christ. Submission and silence are not the only things that the
Pastoral Epistles teach concerning the place of women. They are also called
to sanctification and servanthood. These are to be carried out both in private
and in public. We should be very careful about placing limits upon servanthood. In his book, *Community 101*, Gilbert Bilezikian says that as we face the
hermeneutical risk of trying to adopt the correct theology regarding women
in ministry, we ought to choose the option which will help God's work, not
hinder it.[99] Craig Keener believes that "the Bible permits women's ministry
under normal circumstances but prohibits it in exceptional cases, in which
case we should allow it under most circumstances today."[100] God has
honored the ministry of women; many have done great things for the Lord. I
am not suggesting that we make experience the measuring stick of truth;
what I am saying is that if women are teaching and preaching the truth
effectively for God's glory and kingdom, they have been anointed by God to
do so (Acts 2:17-18). As we have seen, even the apparent restrictive verses of
First Timothy 2 are not sufficient grounds to try to establish a universal principle that women should be restricted in the areas of teaching and exercising
spiritual authority. A holistic look at the teachings of Scripture is necessary to
arrive at a truly biblical theology. God is using women in positions of

---

[99] Gilbert Bilezikian, *Community 101* (Grand Rapids, MI: Zondervan/Willowcreek
Resources, 1997), 82.

[100] Craig S. Keener, "Women in Ministry" (Egalitarian View), *Two Views on Women in
Ministry*. James R. Beck and Craig L. Blomberg, eds. Counterpoints (Grand Rapids,
MI: Zondervan, 2001), 28.

teaching and authority, so those who would seek to silence them should be very careful. They may find, to echo Gamaliel's words, that they are fighting against God (Acts 5:39).

Chapter 8 The Prayer of Gideon

In a seminar I once heard New Testament scholar Dr. Gordon Fee say, "Let me listen to you pray, and I'll write your theology." This statement points out an important fact; a person's prayers are very revealing; they reveal much about the person and his or her perception of God. In this article we will look at a prayer of one of the great Old Testament people of faith, Gideon (Heb. 11:32). Specifically, we will be looking at his prayer that is recorded in Judges 6:36-40. As we consider his prayer, we will look at the historical context of the prayer, Gideon's temperament, the content of his prayer, the attitude in which it was offered, and the reason that it was offered. We will also offer suggestions as to how this prayer may inform the practice of prayer in the contemporary church.

In Judges 6, as in much of the Book of Judges, we find the people of God in trouble. The Eastern peoples, especially the Midianites, were oppressing them (6:2-3). This oppression manifested itself in the ravaging of the Israel-ites' food sources of both crops and animals (6:4). The reason that these terrible events had taken place was because the Israelites were in sin (6:1). These were dark days for Israel. In the midst of these dark days, a glimmer of light shines through as the Israelites cry out to God whom they have offended (6:7). Their turning to the Lord causes the Lord to call a deliverer to free the people from their oppression (6:14,16). The person that the Lord chose for this task was Gideon. In order for us to properly understand and appreciate Gideon's prayer in 6:36-40, it is important to learn what we can about him in the rest of chapter 6.

Judges 6 presents Gideon as a timid individual. In verse 14 the Lord commissioned Gideon to deliver the Israelites out of the hand of Midian.

Gideon's response (6:15), like Moses before him and Jeremiah after him, was to disqualify himself due to perceived personal weaknesses. In verse 16 the Lord affirms that He will give Gideon victory over the Midianites. Gideon's timidity is again seen as he asks the Lord for a sign that it is really the Lord who is speaking to him (6:17). The Lord does give him the sign that he requests. Then in verses 25 and 26 the Lord tells him to destroy his father's idols, which he does. Someone might say that that doesn't sound like something that a timid person would do. It does sound like a brave act. However, as Greg Laurie pointed out on one of his radio programs, Gideon destroyed his father's idols at night when no one was watching. All of this I believe has some bearing on understanding the prayer that we find in 6:36-40. Gideon manifests a timid temperament.

This brings us to the text of the prayer in 6:36-40. We can quickly note that the prayer does not contain any form of direct address (such as "Lord"), nor does it contain any praise or thanksgiving. Gideon's prayer is purely petition. His prayer doesn't attempt to "butter up" the Lord. There is no pretense in the prayer; it is direct and practical. As someone has rightly pointed out Gideon is not seeking the Lord's will; he is seeking confirmation of it. God's will had already been revealed to him (6:14,16). Another point worth mentioning at this juncture is that Gideon is not praying about a moral issue (a matter dealing with personal holiness); he is praying about a ministry, about assuming a leadership role. Part of the reason for his prayer may have been his temperament, but the danger of the task and the implications that this action might have for the Israelites probably also contributed to his requests. He had already established the fact that it was God who was speaking to him (6:17-22); now he wants the Lord to reaffirm the mission that He had given him. Gideon wants to be sure. After the Lord gives him the sign that he requested the first time (6:38), Gideon is apologetic for asking the Lord for yet another sign to confirm His will (6:39). Gideon is very humble about this. Some people may see a lack of faith in Gideon's requests, but one thing that I think needs to be noted is that Gideon felt secure enough in his relationship with God to ask Him these things. In Gideon's case, we are fortunate to be able to see the Lord's response to his requests. While the Lord did not speak to him audibly this time, He did answer him by granting the requests that he had made concerning the fleece (6:37,39). The Lord bore patiently with His timid deliverer. Gideon believed the Lord's answer and went on to be the Lord's deliverer, which resulted in great blessing for the Israelites.

In this article we have seen that Gideon's prayer in 6:36-40 was shaped by his circumstances and his temperament. We have also seen that Gideon's approach to God was very practical, unassuming, and humble. His prayer was effective in that it was answered, and as a result he went forward in faith, which resulted in the deliverance of his people.

The prayer of Gideon is thousands of years old. While we certainly would not want to make it the "model" prayer that all Christians should pray, since it does show some unbelief, it nonetheless has some valuable lessons to teach us regarding the contemporary practice of prayer. The first thing that we can take away from this prayer is that we can be real with God about our fears and reservations. We don't have to pretend with Him, nor should we. A second lesson that we can glean from Gideon's prayer is that if we are weak in faith and we go to God with it, He will encourage our faith, more than once if necessary. This passage speaks especially to those who are going into positions of Christian leadership. If we are called to go into an area of ministry that we have not previously held, that entails great responsibility and will affect many people, God understands our wanting His call and commission to us confirmed. It is important to have this assurance at the outset in order to go forth with conviction.

The story of Gideon is an illustration of the fact that God can take a less than willing, less than faith-filled person and accomplish great things through him or her. A key turning point in bringing this to pass was the prayer that Gideon prayed in 6:36-40, which the Lord in His grace answered.

Chapter 9 Praying for Believers

The New Testament teaches that Christians are brothers and sisters in Christ and should pray for one another (Eph. 6:18; Jas. 5:16). Every genuine believer would affirm that this is a biblical doctrine. But prayer is to be more than a doctrine that we hold; it is to be a discipline that we practice. A thorough reading of the Book of Acts will reveal that the apostolic church practiced prayer. A number of texts show the believers praying with and for one another (Acts 1:14; 4:23-31; 9:40, etc). Most Christians have been asked to pray for a fellow brother or sister in Christ. This usually happens when there is a crisis or need that is near at hand. In Christian charity, we usually comply with the request and pray for the need that has been presented to us. But how do we pray for one another when there is no particular crisis? What kinds of things should we ask for? The apostle Paul provides us with answers to these questions in his prayer in Ephesians 1:15-23. As we consider his prayer, we will look at the various types of prayer that are contained in it, the people for whom it was offered, Paul's attitude in the prayer, the purpose of the prayer, and how this prayer may instruct us in praying for one another. At the conclusion of the consideration of Paul's prayer, I will compare and contrast it with Gideon's prayer in Judges 6:36-40 (see Chapter Eight).

Paul's prayer for the Ephesians is a combination of two types of prayer, thanksgiving and petition. In verse 16 Paul thanks God for his readers; in particular, he thanks God for the spiritual life of the Ephesians. They have a genuine faith in the Lord Jesus and love for all the saints (verse 15). Both their vertical and horizontal relationships seem to be in order. This, however, does not stop Paul from praying for them. On the contrary, even though they are apparently faring well spiritually, Paul proceeds to pray for them. This brings us to the second type of prayer that we find in this passage. In verses 17 and 18, we find Paul petitioning the Lord on their behalf. In verse 17, he asks the Lord to give the Ephesians "the spirit of wisdom and revelation" so that they may know God better. Verse 18 begins a request that stretches right down through the rest of the passage—that the Ephesians would have a more adequate understanding of the hope, inheritance, and power that is theirs in Jesus Christ.

Some of the people that Paul prayed for were Gentiles (2:11; 3:1), Christians that he had some knowledge of (1:15). Paul's attitudes in the prayer can be characterized as both gratitude and concern. He is glad for what they have already attained in Christ (faith and love) and at the same time is concerned that they grow even further in their faith in Christ Jesus. The purpose of this prayer is to invoke God's help in bringing the Ephesian Christian community to a greater level of spiritual maturity. Paul's pastoral heart is evident in this prayer; his prayer is an expression of love for the Ephesians.

Paul's prayer in Ephesians 1:15-23 offers us much by way of instruction as to how we can pray for one another. First of all, there need not be a request from or a problem in another believer's life in order for us to pray for him or her. We ought to pray for one another even when there is no crisis. One thing that we ought to discipline ourselves to do is to thank God for His work that we see in fellow believers' lives. So often we look at the deficiencies and the faults; we all have these, but we ought to look at the positive. The second thing that Paul's prayer teaches us is that we ought to pray for the spiritual lives of other Christians; very often our prayers for one another deal with earthly things. We pray for jobs and money, etc. These things have their place, but let's remember to pray for each other's spiritual health and progress. We all need to know God better and to have a greater under-standing of all that we have in Him. Paul's prayer in Ephesians 1:15-23 could be an ongoing prayer that we pray for one another.

In comparing Paul's New Testament prayer for the Ephesians and Gideon's Old Testament prayer in Judges 6:36-40, a couple of similarities emerge. First of all, both prayers are directed to the one true and living God. The God of Israel is the God of the church. A second characteristic that they both share is that both prayers contain petitions. Petition is a valid form of prayer in both testaments.

There are, however, some differences between Paul's New Testament prayer and Gideon's Old Testament prayer. One contrast between the two prayers is that Gideon is praying about earthly things and Paul is praying about heavenly things. Gideon is seeking God about gaining a military victory in the earthly realm while Paul is praying about gaining a spiritual victory. A second contrast between the two prayers is that Gideon is praying during a crisis situation while Paul does not seem to be praying during a specific time of difficulty. A third difference between the two prayers is that Gideon prays for himself while Paul prays for others. And lastly, Paul seems to pray with much greater confidence than Gideon.

The prayers of Scripture are a great source of inspiration to us. They show us the kinds of things that we can come to God with, and they also show us that we need not necessarily have it all together to come to God. In reality, the very fact that we are coming to God in prayer indicates that we don't have it all together. We have problems, but God has solutions. In going to God in prayer, we are able to bridge the gap between the two. As these two articles on prayer (Chapters Eight and Nine) indicate, our God is concerned about our temporal and our spiritual life.

Chapter 10 Taking the Offering
(For Special Projects or Ministries)

Two of the three words that make up the title of this article can have very different meanings; *take* can mean "to seize or acquire by force"; *offering*, on the other hand, conveys the idea that the giving is voluntary. So there can be a certain tension between the two words. I confess that I have been in services where there was some tension when they were taking the offering. Now, in referring to the offering, I am not referring to the tithe, but to offerings given for special ministry projects.

Money can be a touchy subject, even among God's people. The condition can be further aggravated when certain practices that are contrary to the spirit of Scripture are employed in taking the offering. These practices are abusive and hinder, rather than help, the cause of Christ. While they may produce the desired financial goals, they provoke the saints and mar the Christian testimony for unbelievers who may be present, some of who may already be disposed to believe that the church is only interested in money.

Let me say at the outset that I believe in offerings. God's people should finance the work of the Lord. Ministry does have some expenses. Believers should be aware of this and be taught to give. Both the Old and New Testaments contain instructions about giving. Offerings, however, are not the problem; it is the methods employed by some in taking them. In a day when financial accountability is a major concern for the church, I think that attention should be given not only to how funds are spent but also to how they are raised. I am sure that the Lord is concerned about both of these areas. What follows is a brief description of two methods of taking the offering that can be abusive.

The Autocratic Method

When this method is employed, the individual responsible for taking the offering dictates the amount that everyone should give. The amount is usually high, and he sometimes indicates that he has received the figure from the Lord.

A number of years ago, we had a couple of men visit the mid-week Bible study at our church. They told us of their experience in another church. In this other church, a man got up and said that God told him that everyone was supposed to put two hundred dollars (or some such amount) in the offering. Now I was not there, but assuming that this report is true, I don't think that the man was hearing from God.

To begin with, I don't think that God would require everyone to give the same dollar figure. God knows that we do not all have the same financial capabilities. Two hundred dollars would not be an unrealistic figure for a top executive who makes two thousand dollars a week. However, such a figure would be almost totally out of the question for a student or a factory worker who receives only a few hundred dollars a week. While we are all called to sacrifice, we are not all called to equal dollar contributions. The Lord does not reckon money as man does; remember the widow's mite (see Mark 12). Jesus said that she put in even more than the rich, who gave large sums, because she gave out of her poverty while they gave out of their abundance. The autocrat may repeatedly punctuate his appeal for money with promises of God's blessings, but he has already violated one of God's principles of giving. The Scripture declares that God loves a cheerful giver (2 Cor. 9:7). The autocrat has taken the joy out by oppressing many of God's people with his exorbitant requests for funds. Worst of all is the fact that he claims that God is the one who is requiring this; thus, he makes God appear very oppressive.

The Auctioneer's Method

You know the type I'm talking about. The person who is in charge of taking the offering gets up and says, "Who'll start us off with a thousand dollars, a thousand dollars, yes, I see that hand. God bless you. Somebody else…I need twenty more people to give a thousand dollars." Then he scales the amount down and repeats the process until he gets the appropriate number of contributors for that amount, and on it goes. It is true auctioneers usually up the amount, but there is a similarity in sound between the auctioneer and his religious counterpart as they conduct business. Now this method does in some sense recognize differing abilities to give but does so only after pressing for the highest possible donation. I also wonder if this method violates the spirit of Matthew 6 where we are told not to do our acts of righteousness before men. When this method is employed, those who respond to the requests for the larger amounts are praised before men; eventually, before the plate is passed, all are encouraged to give whatever they can. Those who have not been able to commit to the higher amounts may feel as though they are second-rate citizens. I can't see the apostle Peter or any of the other apostles taking an offering in this way. Like the autocrat, the auctioneer can claim that God gave him the figures, but I doubt it. There is no record of the New Testament church taking up any offering like this.

To be sure, those who employ the previously mentioned methods are few. The money is for a noble cause—the work of the ministry—but does the end justify the means? I think that as the church we need to give careful consideration to the methods that are used in raising funds. We need to ask the question: are we simply encouraging people to give, or have we crossed the line into manipulation? The financial giving of God's people is to be an act of worship, and as with all other things it is to be done to the glory of God (1 Cor.10:31).

Chapter 11 Looking at the Past, Learning for the Present

> He broke into pieces the bronze snake Moses had made, for up to that time the Israelites had been burning incense to it… (2 Kings 18:4).

In First Corinthians 10, the apostle Paul writes that as believers in Jesus we should learn from the experiences of the people of Israel as recorded in the Old Testament. The above-mentioned Scripture from Second Kings 18 is one such text from which we can learn. This Scripture records an event that took place in the southern kingdom of Judah during the time of the kings. This was a turbulent time spiritually; at times the people were zealous for the Lord, and at other times they were not. The spiritual temperature of the people was in some measure dependent on the spirituality of the king at that time. At this particular time Hezekiah was king. He was a godly man who sought to do what was right in God's sight. Under his leadership a number of religious reforms were introduced. We are told that "he removed the high places, smashed the sacred stones and cut down the Asherah poles" (2 Kings 18:4). The breaking of the bronze snake was also a part of his religious reform. In order to better understand the significance of this act, we need to go further back in Israelite history.

The bronze snake dates back to the time of Moses; we find it mentioned in Numbers 21. At that time the Israelites were grumbling and complaining against God and against Moses. They accused God and Moses of bringing them out of Egypt to die in the desert. They also complained that there was no water and no bread, and they spoke with displeasure of God's gracious provision of manna (Num. 21:4-5). Because of their sinful behavior, the Lord sent venomous snakes among the people to bite them, and many Israelites died as a result of the snake bites (Num. 21:6). Once this began to happen, the people went to Moses, acknowledged that they had sinned, and asked Moses to petition the Lord to take the snakes away from them (Num. 21:7). Interestingly enough, the Lord did not take the snakes away, but He did do something else. The Lord instructed Moses to make a bronze snake and put it on a pole; if anyone was bitten by a snake and looked at the bronze snake, he or she would live (Num. 21:8).

There are a number of significant things about the bronze snake that we should note at this point. First, the bronze snake was God's idea. The people had asked for the removal of the snakes (Num. 21:7), not for a bronze snake. Neither Moses nor the people could say that they had come up with the idea of the bronze snake; the bronze snake was totally God's idea. Second, the bronze snake was crafted by Moses. Moses was a man of God, one of the most recognized and revered leaders in Israelite history. He made what God had ordered. Third, the bronze snake was used by God to bless His people at this one particular point in time. Specifically, it was used by God to spare people's lives. This is the object that Hezekiah smashed. *What was he thinking? Didn't he know the history of the bronze snake?*

Yes, I believe that Hezekiah knew the history of the snake. What Hezekiah was thinking was—idolatry. Everything that the king did away with in Second Kings 18:4 had to do with idolatry. We can certainly understand that the high places, sacred stones, and Asherah poles were idolatrous, and we would approve of their destruction. But what does the bronze snake have to do with idolatry?

Many years transpired between the time of Moses and the time of the kings. The Israelites had kept the bronze snake, crafted by Moses, from the time of its creation in Numbers 21 until the time of Second Kings 18. Not only had they kept the snake, but, as Second Kings 18:4 tells us, they were burning incense to it. Herein was the problem: the Israelites took something from the past that was ordained of God, that was brought into being at the hands of a man of God, that God used to bless His people; they brought it into the present and gave it a place that God never intended it to have. They actually came to the place where they confused the bronze snake with God Himself! They were burning incense to the snake; they were worshipping it! There is a word of warning here for us. History is good, and we need to recognize its importance and learn from it, as Paul reminds us in First Corinthians 10, but we also need to be on our guard that we do not let history become a snare to us. We need to be careful that we do not try to bring into the present something that God intended only for the past. We also need to be careful that we do not honor something that God blessed in the past to the point where we blur the distinction between the method, or tool, that God used and God Himself. If we fall prey to either of these things, we can become guilty of idolatry. Because the method, or tool, has such a close connection to God in our minds, it may, at times, be difficult for us to discern the idolatry. If we become aware that we have made something into an idol, we need to do what Hezekiah did; we need to get rid of the idol (see also 1 John 5:21). Let us not hold on to it and be held back. As time marches on, let us move forward with God, the living God, worshipping and honoring Him alone—and let us be found walking in obedience to His Word and His Spirit.

Chapter 12   **The Next Generation?**

> I brought you up out of Egypt, and I led you for forty years in
> the desert to give you the land of the Amorites. I also raised up
> prophets from among your sons and Nazirites from among
> your young men. Is this not true, people of Israel? declares the
> Lord. But you made the Nazirites drink wine and commanded
> the prophets not to prophesy (Amos 2:10-12).

This is a very interesting portion of Scripture; in it the Lord, through the
prophet Amos, speaks to His people Israel and reminds them of what He has
done for the nation. In verse 10 the Lord says that He brought them out of
Egypt. They needed a Savior; they needed freedom from their oppressors,
and the Lord was their deliverer. In the Book of Exodus, Moses provides us
with a rather detailed account of how the Lord delivered His people (Exod.
7-12). This event was a very significant moment in the life of the nation.
However, the Lord's activity in the life of His people did not end with the
Exodus. After He delivered them from Egyptian bondage, the Lord stayed
with Israel; He led them for forty years in the desert. He led them by a pillar
of cloud by day and a pillar of fire by night (Exod. 13:21-22). During the
course of this time, He also fed them; He provided them with manna to eat
the whole time that they were in the desert (Exod. 16:35). The Lord stayed
with His people even though at times they were less than grateful. Scripture
tells us in a number of places about their complaints and their sins (Exod.
16:2-8; 17:1-7; 32:1-35). God stayed with His people because He wanted to
bring them into an inheritance; His leading was purposeful and intentional.
He brought them out to bring them in (Deut. 6:23). In verse 11, the Lord also

says that He raised up prophets and Nazarites from among their young people. All of the emphasis thus far has been on what God had done.

In verse 12, the emphasis changes. Now the Lord speaks about what Israel did with reference to His work of raising up prophets and Nazirites from among their young people. He says that Israel made the Nazirites drink wine and commanded the prophets not to prophesy. God had called and raised up spiritually dedicated and gifted people and the larger community, *the community of God's people*, had shut them down. The Nazirite vow dates back to the time of Moses; it was a voluntary vow, and we find a record of what it entailed in Numbers 6. Nazirites were not to drink wine or other fermented drinks or eat grapes or raisins; they were not to partake of anything that came from the grapevine (Num. 6:3-4). They were also not to cut their hair while they were under a Nazirite vow, nor were they to go near a dead body, even if a close family member died (Num. 6:5-8). God raised up people with this special consecration and dedication, and the Israelites had made them drink wine. In other words, they compromised them; they caused them to break their special dedication. God also raised up prophets, inspired speakers who had His Word, His message, and the people told the prophets not to deliver the Word of the Lord. How awful! How could they, the people of God, do such a thing? Why would they do such a thing? I think that there are a couple of possible explanations as to why Israel put down what God had raised up.

One reason why Israel may have undermined the Nazirites and prophets is because of unbelief. The text says that God raised these consecrated and gifted individuals up from the sons of the people. The nation may not have received them because they were young or because they were known. "We know where they are from; we know their families; we know their sins and their shortcomings. Surely God would not call them!" This ties in with what Jesus said in the New Testament. He said that a prophet is not without honor except in his own hometown and in his own house (Matt. 13:57). Israel may also have resisted the Nazirites and prophets that God raised up because consecrated and gifted people like them make others uncomfortable. The dedication and zeal of a Nazirite or prophet could be very convicting to a people who know that they are not following the Lord as they should (they definitely do not want to hear from the prophet what God thinks of them). In an attempt to ease their own sense of guilt, they undermined the spirituality of the committed. These are a couple of possible explanations of why Israel treated the Nazirites and prophets as they did.

We need to ask ourselves, have we done, or are we now doing, the same thing? As God is raising up a new generation of spiritually dedicated and gifted people, are we discouraging those that God is calling? Don't dismiss this idea too quickly. Do we fail to believe that God could use our sons or daughters or other young people who are in our churches? Or are we compromising them by encouraging them to continue in their faith but at the same time urging them not to become too fanatical: "Don't go crazy with this." How many future apostles, prophets, evangelists, pastors, teachers, and missionaries will never answer the call of God because they have not been encouraged by the church? In the twenty-first century we have an additional reason for discouraging them; serving the Lord doesn't tie in with the American dream. "Don't go that way; you can't make any money serving the Lord!" May the Lord help us to recognize who He is calling, and may we do everything that we can to help them on their way to answer the call and follow through with it. God's way is the best way for them, and every generation needs good Christian leaders. May what the Lord said to Israel in this text never be said of us.

Chapter 13   Who Is Jesus?

During the course of His earthly ministry Jesus Christ asked His disciples who people were saying that He was (Matt. 16:13). His disciples responded with a number of different answers, including John the Baptist, Elijah, and Jeremiah (Matt. 16:14). What their answers indicate is that the people had various opinions about who Jesus was and that everyone's perception of Jesus was not the same. This has been the case from the time of Jesus' earthly ministry up to the present day. There has been, and is, a division among the people concerning Him (John 7:43). People's perceptions of Jesus are varied, and this holds true for the average person on the street and the trained theologian. His name is familiar to most even though He may not be "well known." The average person on the street may say that Jesus is a good example or a good teacher. The trained theologian will offer a more detailed analysis of who He is. Within the last century and a half, there have been three quests for the historic Jesus.[101] In all of these, the attempt has been made to answer the question, "Who is this?" In the remainder of this article, I shall attempt to answer this question as it relates to Jesus' person and His work of redemption. The main sources that I will use in this work will be the writings of the New Testament, for as Warfield rightly points out, "The Lord's person is a matter of revelation, not human thought."[102] We must see what God has said about His Son in His Word, through His inspired writers (2 Tim. 3:16; 2 Pet. 1:20-21).

---

[101] Ben Witherington III, *The Jesus Quest: The Third Search for the Jew of Nazareth*, expanded edition (Downers Grove, IL: InterVarsity Press, 1994), preface 9-13.

[102] Benjamin B. Warfield, *The Person and Work of Christ*, ed. by Samuel G. Craig (Phillipsburg, NJ: Presbyterian and Reformed Publishing Company, 1950), 37.

In studying the person of Jesus, one of the major issues that one must come to terms with is the seemingly contradictory pictures that one finds of Him in the New Testament. In some texts, Jesus appears to be a man; in others He appears to be God. In some texts, He is explicitly called a man (1 Tim. 2:5), and in others He is called God (John 20:28; Heb. 1:8). And these apparent contradictions are not even the conflicting views of two different writers, for we find the same writer speaking of both Jesus' humanity and His deity (see, for example, 1 Tim. 2:5 and Rom. 9:5). Sometimes a given author will even refer to Jesus' humanity and deity in the course of the same book. Paul does this in the same passage in Philippians 2.[103] It is an indisputable fact that the New Testament presents Jesus as both God and man.

That Jesus possessed attributes of humanity can be seen in a number of ways in the New Testament. As Hodge points out, Jesus was born of a woman, and His body went through all of the ordinary developmental stages that are typical for human beings.[104] This is true. In Luke 2 we find record of the birth of Jesus as a baby (Luke 2:7). Later in the same chapter, we find the account of an incident in the life of the boy Jesus when He was twelve years old (Luke 2:42). As we move to Luke 3, we find the beginning of the account of Jesus' life as a man. Hodge also points out that during the course of His earthly life Jesus was subject to all of the affections of the human body, including "pain, pleasure, hunger, thirst, fatigue, suffering and death."[105] In John 4, we find the record of some of Jesus' physical needs, He was tired (4:6) and thirsty (4:7). John 19 supplies us with an account of His suffering and death.

The reality of His humanity is further documented by the fact that He could touch and be touched. Examples of Jesus touching others are found in His healing of a leper (Matt. 8:1-4), His healing of Peter's mother-in-law

---

[103] Ibid, 39.

[104] Charles Hodge, *Systematic Theology*, ed. Edward N. Gross, abridged ed. (Grand Rapids, MI: Baker Book House, 1988), 354.

[105] Ibid.

(Matt. 8:15), and the healing of the ear of the high priest's servant (Luke 22:51). Accounts of His being touched include that of the woman who wet Jesus' feet with her tears and dried them with her hair (Luke 7:38), the disciples touching Him (1 John 1:1), and His being struck by the soldiers (John 19:3). He was a real human being when He came in the flesh (1 John 4:2; John 1:14).

Added to all of this are the direct statements in the New Testament that Jesus was human. These affirmations are found on the lips of both His friends and His foes in the sacred Scripture (John 9:16, 24; Acts 2:22, 1 Tim. 2:5). The clear testimony of the Scriptures is that Jesus was a man. He possessed all of the attributes or characteristics of humanity, except that He was without sin (1 John 3:5).

The Scriptures also teach that Jesus Christ is God. This truth is woven throughout the New Testament. As Davis writes, "The Deity of Jesus Christ in scripture is demonstrated with reference to divine titles, divine attributes, divine actions and New Testament texts that specifically state an equality or identity between God and Christ."[106] This summary statement demonstrates just how extensive the scriptural evidence for the deity of Christ is.

Hodge gives us a list of divine titles applied to Jesus Christ, including the great God, God over all, and the Lord of lords and King of kings.[107] These titles are found in texts written by the apostles Paul and John. They are found respectively in Titus 2:13, Romans 9:5, and Revelation 17:14; 19:16.

In addition to the divine titles there are also divine attributes and actions that are applied to Christ. Davis supplies us with a list of them. The attributes include eternity (John 1:1; Rev. 22:13) and universal authority (Matt. 28:18). The divine activities include creation (John 1:3; Col. 1:16; Heb. 1:2); forgiveness of sins (Mark 2:5-7); power to raise the dead (John 5:21; 11:25);

---

[106] John Jefferson Davis, *Handbook of Basic Bible Texts: Every Key Passage for the Study of Doctrine &Theology* (Grand Rapids, MI: Zondervan/Academic, 1984), 68-69.

[107] Hodge, 354.

and the judgment of humanity (Matt. 25:31-32).[108]

Even more conclusive evidence of the fact that the New Testament teaches that Jesus is God is that He is specifically called God in the New Testament. He is called God by Thomas (John 20:28); by Paul (Rom. 9:5); by John (John 1:1,14); and, in the context of Hebrews 1, by God the Father (Heb. 1:8).

The scriptural revelation that Jesus Christ is fully God and fully man is a difficult concept to grasp. In an effort to clarify this truth, a couple of early church councils spelled out in some detail the finer points of this doctrine. This subject was dealt with at both the Council of Nicaea and the Council of Chalcedon.

The *Nicene Creed* stressed that Jesus is "of one substance with the Father."[109] By this the fathers intended to indicate that Jesus was of the same essence as the Father. They also stressed that He was "begotten not made," meaning that He was not a creation.[110] This creed also affirmed that He became man, thus implying that He pre-existed. All of this was spelled out to counter some heretical teachings that were around at the time.

The *Definition of Chalcedon* also went into detail to clearly spell out the doctrine of Christ. In addition to affirming some of the same truths as the Creed of Nicaea, namely, His absolute divinity ("complete in Godhead," "truly God," "of one substance with the Father"); pre-existence ("begotten of the Father before the ages"); and His humanity ("complete in manhood," "truly man," "one substance with us"), it went on to spell out some further specifics regarding these two natures.[111] The creed declared that Christ's two natures are "without confusion, without change, without division, and

---

[108] Davis, 70-72.

[109] The *Nicene Creed*, http://www.reformed.org/documents/index.html (accessed June 2009).

[110] Ibid.

[111] The *Definition of Chalcedon*, http://www.reformed.org/documents/index.html? mainframe=http://www.reformed.org/documents/chalcedon.html (accessed July 2010).

without separation."[112] They stressed that the distinctions did not nullify the union and that Christ was one person.

Jesus, the God-man, came into world, with a body that was prepared for Him (Heb. 10:5) to save sinners (1 Tim. 1:15). He accomplished this salvation through the sacrifice of Himself. What is, therefore, important for us to understand is the meaning of the word *sacrifice*, because that is how the first-century believers perceived the work of Jesus on the cross.[113] Warfield tells us that the sacrifice of Jesus was looked upon as a ransoming.[114] The word, *ransom*, means "to buy out" or to "secure release by the payment of a price."[115] So while Jesus gave His life for us, His work was directed to God to affect Him.[116] Those who put their faith in Jesus receive pardon for their sins and the gift of eternal life because God has accepted Jesus' sacrifice.

I am thankful for Jesus Christ and the salvation that He has secured for me. I am also thankful for His Presence in my life and for the infinite patience that He yet shows toward me. He has been a source of strength and has helped me to trust Him with the church that I serve and the ministry that I have. I found Jesus to be what the Scriptures declare concerning Him, that He is a patient, pardoning, and powerful God.

---

[112] Ibid.

[113] Warfield, 391.

[114] Ibid, 334.

[115] Ibid, 330, 336.

[116] Ibid, 407.

Chapter 14 Jesus: Model for the Church's Public Ministry

The appearance of Jesus Christ in human history some 2,000 years ago was an event of epic proportion. His life and ministry have left an indelible mark upon the world. In spite of all attempts in the past and in the present to suppress, ignore, and extinguish the memory of His life and teachings, He remains with us. He will not go away. The truth is that He will remain forever (Heb. 13:8). The world has not, indeed cannot, remain the same because of His coming.

His birth marked the beginning of the fulfilling of the Old Testament prophecies concerning the Messiah (Isa. 7:14; Matt. 1:22-23; Mic. 5:2; Matt. 2:3-6). As His life and ministry unfolded, more and more of the ancient prophecies were fulfilled, thus confirming the fact that God's Messiah had appeared. He for whom the Jews had hoped and prayed had come. Unfortunately, not all recognized this truth. Jesus was rejected by most of the religious leaders of His day. Nonetheless, He repeatedly said that He was sent by God (John 5:23, 36-37; 8:16,18). He stated that He always pleased God (John 8:29). He claimed that His words were the words of God (John 7:16; 14:24) and that His works were the works of God (John 5:36). On one occasion, He said that to see Him was to see the Father (John 14:9). And just before His execution, when pointedly asked if He was the Christ, He responded that He was (Mark 14:61). Truly, God had come near.

There is an old saying that "a picture is worth a thousand words." There is an element of truth in that statement. One thing that the coming of Jesus Christ did was to make God more understandable. The people of Jesus' day not only heard the words of God, but they heard them from the lips of God Himself. They were privileged to see how God conducted Himself in a sinful world in relation to sinful people. The apostle John tells us that "grace and truth came through Jesus Christ" (John 1:17). In Jesus, the Old Testament revelation of God as being compassionate, gracious, slow to anger, and forgiving (Exod. 34:6-7) was graphically seen. We, these many centuries later, reap the benefit of this revelation as we read the record of it preserved for us in the New Testament. There is no doubt that Jesus has given us a better picture of who God is. The writer to the Hebrews indicates as much when he contrasts how God revealed Himself in past (in the Old Testament) by the prophets and how He revealed Himself in the New Testament by His Son (Heb. 1:1-3). The revelation in the past was largely partial and through a middle man, a prophet. The revelation through His Son, though veiled, was unparalleled and direct. God was revealing Himself.

It is widely acknowledged that Christ revealed the person of God. A fact that may be less recognized is that He models for the church what its public ministry should be. To be sure, there is a limit to this comparison of Christ's ministry and the ministry of the church; namely, that the church is not sent to provide eternal salvation as Jesus was. Nonetheless, He serves, or should serve, as a model for the church both in the ministries it carries on and in how it conducts them. In this article, we shall look at Jesus as the model for the public ministry of the church.

Before proceeding further, we need to address two issues. First, are there sufficient biblical grounds for believing that Jesus' ministry should be the model for the public ministry of the church? And second, we need to define what we mean by public ministry.

As to the question of whether there are sufficient biblical grounds for believing that Jesus' ministry should be a model for the ministry of the church, it should be noted that from the early days of His public ministry, Jesus was calling people to Himself. In Matthew 4 we see Him call Peter and Andrew (4:18-19). His invitation to them was "Come, follow me" (Matt.

4:19). A couple of verses later, we find Him calling another pair of brothers, James and John, to Himself (Matt. 4:21). Later in the first gospel we also find Him calling the tax collector, Matthew, to Himself with the words, "Follow me" (Matt. 9:9). There is a reason for these invitations, and it is more than just companionship. There is a hint of the purpose in His call to the fishermen Peter and Andrew. "Come, follow me," Jesus said, "and I will make you fishers of men" (Matt. 4:19). There is a task that He wants them to engage in, but He needs to train them for it. He will train them through instruction and example. The specifics of this task are laid out more fully in other texts in the gospels.

In His calling of the Twelve to be apostles, it is stated that the reason He called them to Himself was, first of all, to be with Him, and then so that He might send them out in ministry, specifically preaching and driving out demons (Mark 3:14-15). In Matthew 10, Jesus expands upon the two ministries that were mentioned in Mark 3. In addition to preaching and driving out demons, He tells His disciples to heal the sick, raise the dead, and cleanse the leper (Matt. 10:7-8). These were the types of things that Jesus Himself was doing. He gave His disciples authority and sent them out to do the same (Matt. 10:1, 7-8), and they did just that. Mark tells us in his gospel that "they went out and preached that people should repent. They drove out many demons and anointed many sick people with oil and healed them" (Mark 6:12-13). Now, lest it be thought that Jesus intended His ministry to serve as a model only to the apostles, two things should be noted. First, just prior to His sending the Twelve out in Matthew 10, we are told that Jesus was engaged in the ministry of teaching, preaching, and healing (Matt. 9:35). Immediately afterward, we are told that He looked upon the crowds of needy people and asked His disciples to pray that God would send out laborers into His harvest (Matt. 9:36-37). The text indicates that there is a need for more workers, more than those who heard Him speak at that time. There is additional scriptural support for this idea. The second thing that we can see which supports this idea is that Jesus appointed seventy-two others and sent them out two by two with a similar mission (Luke 10:1,9,17). This establishes the fact that Jesus' ministry was a model. That is, the things that Jesus did, others were to do after Him. But these people all lived during the time of Jesus, the first century A.D. The question may be raised—are there any indications that Jesus saw His ministry as being a model for subsequent generations of believers? Are the ministries that He engaged in to continue throughout the life of the church?

The answer to these questions is, yes. Jesus did see His ministry as continuing after His earthly life and the lives of His apostles. These ministries were to continue through His church. Evidence in support of this view can be found in a number of texts in the New Testament. One thing that is clear from the teaching of Jesus is that He had very big plans for the ministry that He had begun. Jesus preached the gospel (Mark 1:15), and He declared that this message would be preached in all the world before the end would come (Matt. 24:14). Since the ministry of Jesus and the apostles was concentrated in the East, it is necessary that there be others to carry it to the West. In addition, since all people are sinners, there would always be a need for each generation to have its own witness to the gospel. Both geographic and generational factors point to the need for a continuing ministry. In Acts 1:8, Jesus again indicated that His mission was a worldwide one. The gospel was to begin in Jerusalem and reach to the ends of the earth. Three of the Great Commission passages also indicate that the message is to cover the globe (Matt. 28:19; Mark 16:15; and Luke 24:47). Matthew's account speaks of the timelessness of the preaching in that the preaching is to continue "to the very end of the age" (Matt. 28:20).

So the preaching ministry is to go on, but what about the healing and deliverance ministries of Jesus? Are they to continue? The answer to these questions is also, yes. The Great Commission passage in Mark 16:17-18 includes these miraculous elements as well. Now I know that there is some debate about whether this portion of Mark should be considered canonical Scripture. But even if it is not considered canonical, the New Testament makes it clear that the early church did these things. They engaged in healing (Jas. 5:14-15; Acts 3:6-9; 5:15-16; 9:17-18; 28:8-9), and exorcism (Acts 5:16; 16:16-18). And these ministries were not limited to the apostles. In Acts 8 we see these things taking place in Samaria in Philip's ministry (Acts 8:6-7). While it is true that all who engaged in these works were first-century people, the Lord has seen fit to provide for the continuation of these ministries through the gifts of the Spirit (1 Cor. 12). So Jesus' ministry is to serve as a model for the church's public ministry. Having established that, we must now define what we mean by public ministry.

When I was a student at Gordon-Conwell's Center for Urban Ministerial Education in a class on the public ministry of the church, Dr. Eldin Villafané defined public ministry as "ministry to the strangers and other"; it is "to all people in society without distinction or qualification." It is ministry, "out there." In his book, *Love, Acceptance & Forgiveness*, Jerry Cook talks about the concept of the church as a field; in some people's minds this means that all of the work of the church is to take place on the church grounds. Cook reminds us that Jesus said that "the field is the world" (Matt. 13:38).[117] Public ministry is to the public. Having now seen that Jesus' ministry is the model for the public ministry of the church, and having defined public ministry, let us now turn our attention to some specifics that we will need to incorporate into the public ministry of the church if we are truly to follow Jesus' model and be successful in ministry.

The first principle of Jesus' ministry that we need to adopt is the principle of incarnation. Scripture is very clear that the God/man Jesus Christ took on a human body. This was prophesied in the Old Testament (Isa. 7:14) and fulfilled in the New Testament (Matt. 1:22-25). This truth is affirmed time and again in the New Testament (John 1:14; Phil. 2:7-8; 1 Tim. 3:16; Heb. 2:14; and 1 John 4:2). Dr. Villafané describes it this way: "It is the 'Holy Other' pitching

---

[117] Jerry Cook, with Stanley Baldwin, *Love, Acceptance & Forgiveness* (Ventura, CA: Regal Books, 1979), 37-38.

God's tent among us in the person of Jesus Christ" (John 1:14; Phil. 2:5-11).[118] The fact that the incarnation is referred to repeatedly in Scripture is an indication of its importance. Certainly God coming to earth in human form for an extended period of time is significant simply because of who He is.

But there is another aspect of the incarnation of vital importance to the public ministry of the church that may be easily overlooked. That is the issue of context. When Jesus came into the world and took on a body, He placed Himself in a particular context. Dr. Villafané says, "Contextualization means many things to many people; the best image and the clearest biblical insight into its meaning is the incarnation."[119] In taking on human form, Jesus placed Himself in a particular place at a particular time to carry on His ministry. This may seem like a small point, but we dare not minimize it. There is great wisdom in this approach. Robert Linthicum says, "When Jesus sought to win humanity to God, he became one of us, lived among us, voluntarily took upon himself our limitations..."[120] This is one of the first steps in building effective ministry, being among the people that you are trying to reach. This geographic alignment with the people does a number of things; it establishes a point of contact, making you available to the people and the people to you. Linthicum, speaking of the ministry of Jesus, says, "The unique power of Jesus Christ in his work of redemption among us was that he became one with us. Our God was not an absentee God..."[121] The key point that I would like to highlight from this quotation is that God is not an absentee God. If God thought it necessary to be physically present among the people He wanted to reach, how can we expect to carry on effective ministry unless we draw near to the people we want to reach? As the world "progresses," it becomes more impersonal. We live in a world where we are more often a

---

[118] Eldin Villafané, *Seek the Peace of the City: Reflections on Urban Ministry* (Grand Rapids, MI: Wm. B. Eerdmans Publishing Company, 1995), 81.

[119] Ibid.

[120] Robert Linthicum, *Empowering the Poor: Community Organizing Among the City's 'Rag, Tag, and Bobtail'* (Monrovia, CA: MARC/World Vision International, 1991), 35.

[121] Ibid.

number than a name or a face. That is the way of the world; we as the church must resist that mentality. We need to be reminded of this. John Stott writes, "It comes more natural to us to shout the gospel at people from a distance than to involve ourselves deeply in their lives to think ourselves into their culture and their problems, and to feel with them in their pains."[122] It may be more natural to seek to minister at a distance, but it is more necessary to minister in the context of the people that you seek to reach. Robert Linthicum also says that we must be present with people in order to do effective ministry.[123] To paraphrase a couple of points in Linthicum's theology of urban ministry, the church needs to be in the geographic location with the people that they are trying to reach, and it also needs to be with them as it incarnates itself.[124] There needs to be both presence and participation. The principle of incarnation is vital. We need to be among the people as Jesus was. It is hard to lay hands on the sick if they are far removed from where you are. Context is important. But there is another important aspect concerning contextualized ministry that we need to be aware of.

Contextualized ministry is costly. We can see this in the experience of Jesus Christ. In Philippians 2, the apostle Paul tells us what Jesus did in the incarnation (2:6-8). He temporarily set aside some of the benefits of heaven and who He was and adopted the liabilities of earth. He left a perfect place to come to an imperfect place. He traded peace and praise for problems. He moved out of the comfort zone. It is one thing to lose wealth, position, and power; it is another thing to set it aside in order to take up suffering, pain, and conflict, but that is what Jesus did. There is a kind of double cost involved in His coming to minister. The apostle Paul expressed this double cost when he wrote that Jesus was rich but that He left His riches and became poor so that we might become rich through His poverty (2 Cor. 8:9).

---

[122] John Stott, *Christian Mission in the Modern World* (Downers Grove, IL: InterVarsity Press, 1975), 25.

[123] Linthicum, 39.

[124] Ibid, 21,33.

In his book, *Journey to the Center of the City*, Randy White speaks about "downward mobility."[125] That is exactly what Jesus Christ engaged in. Our society is very interested in upward mobility, bigger houses, better cars, more cash, and more prestige. It knows very little about taking a step down. As the church of Jesus Christ, we must be willing to take that step down as our Master did. Taking that step may mean leaving a very promising or lucrative career, or having advanced theological degrees and serving in a storefront church in a tough area of town. It is a laying down of one's life. As Dr. Villa-fané mentioned in one of his class lectures, all significant ministry is costly. Having looked at the principle of incarnation and seen the importance of context and its cost, let us now give our attention to the next principle of Jesus' ministry that the church needs to employ in its public ministry.

The next principle is the principle of intentionality. Jesus Christ came into the world and was present with humanity, but He was not merely an observer of humanity's plight. Jesus made contact with His world; He actively engaged it. He was not passive. On one occasion He said that He "came to seek and to save what was lost" (Luke 19:10). In the gospels we find Him repeatedly initiating contact with people. He went to religious services in the synagogue (Mark 1:21; 3:1), and He attended social events such as a wedding feast (John 2). He went to public places, such as the Temple (Mark 11:11), and to private gatherings such as a dinner in a Pharisee's house (Luke 7:36). He openly proclaimed His message (Mark 1:14-15) and traveled around spreading His teaching (Matt. 4:23). He taught in the synagogue (Luke 4:14-30) and in the open air (Matthew chapters 5-7). He spoke to individuals such as Zacchaeus (Luke 19:5), Nicodemus (John 3), the woman at the well (John 4), and the invalid at the pool of Bethesda (John 5). He also addressed large groups (John 6; Matt. chapters 5-7). His speaking was not strictly discourse or lecture; He drew people into conversation (John 4).

We also find that on a number of occasions He invited individuals to

---

[125] Randy White, *Journey to the Center of the City: Making a Difference in an Urban Neighborhood* (Downers Grove, IL: InterVarsity Press, 1996), 23.

follow Him. He called two brothers, Simon and Andrew, to Himself (Mark 1:16-17). A couple of verses later, He called another set of brothers, James and John (Mark 1:19-20). He called Philip (John 1:43) and extended the same invitation to a tax collector by the name of Matthew (Matt. 9:9). In Mark 3:13-14, we see Him calling the individuals that we have just mentioned plus some others. Now, some may argue that the Twelve are a special group called for the ministry, and in one sense that is true. But the invitation to come to and follow Him seems to have been open to all (Matt. 11:28; John 7:37). Those who did come to Him, whom He touched, He changed; examples of these include Zacchaeus (Luke 19), the woman at the well (John 4), and the demoniac (Mark 5). In each of these cases, the people went out and began to minister. This is God's plan, not only for those who lived in the first century A.D. during the earthly ministry of Jesus, but for all who would come to Him up until the end of time (Matt. 28:18-20). So, Jesus actively engaged His world. Through the intentionality of His ministry, He sought people out, and interestingly enough, we find that people also sought Him out. People who sought Him out include the woman with the flow of blood, Jairus the synagogue ruler (Luke 8), and the woman with the demon-possessed daughter (Matt. 15:21-28). People with problems knew who to go to. Certainly His ministry successes were a major reason for the people seeking Him out, but the fact that He was in the community and His ministry was known also contributed to the people's pursuit of Him. Our problem in the church today is that we are less intentional. We wait around for the world to come to us while we major in giving our "silent witness." Our hopes that the world will come to our doors often don't materialize. Thus, many people go on hurting and headed for hell. We need to be more intentional. However, we need to be careful about how we express this intentionality.

Jesus had a mission that He carried out in the world, but He did it based on a consecration to God. He had the approval of God (Matt. 3:17), the anointing of God (Luke 4:18-19), and I believe that He had God's blessing because He lived a life that was devoted to God. This devotion can be seen in

His practice of prayer (Luke 5:16) and obedience (John 8:29). He prayed before making major decisions. In Luke 6:12 we see Him spending the night in prayer before calling the Twelve. He prayed in the Garden of Gethsemane when He was struggling with the will of God (Matt. 26:36-46). But prayer was not something that He engaged in only when confronted with a decision or a crisis. Luke 5:16 tells us that "Jesus often withdrew to lonely places and prayed." It was this private practice of prayer that guided and empowered His public ministry. Jesus taught by example that there needs to be a spiritual investment in order to carry on an effective public ministry. He also taught this by direct instruction. In Mark 9, the disciples were faced with a demon-possessed boy that they were not able to set free. Jesus delivered the boy. The disciples later asked Jesus why they were not able to drive it out. Jesus reply was, "This kind can come out only by prayer" (Mark 9:29). He taught them to pray for God's glory, God's kingdom, God's will, their physical needs, and their spiritual needs (Matt. 6:9-13). Jesus even told His disciples to pray for people who persecute them (Matt. 5:44). Prayer was to inform all of their life. One of the great needs of the contemporary church is the need for more prayer. We can go and engage our world, doing the "work of the ministry," but if we lack prayer we will not be as productive as we could be. We may even come off as shallow or self-righteous.

Another vital aspect of Jesus' spirituality was His knowledge and command of Scripture. We know that He read it, for we see Him doing so in the synagogue at Nazareth (Luke 4). He had a familiarity with it that enabled Him to bring it forth when necessary. He quoted it when He was tempted (Matt. 4), and He also brought it forth in His public ministry, presumably without the use of a scroll (Mark 7:6-7; 12:10-11). Some may argue that Jesus was God so He knew the Word. That, however, does not excuse us from applying ourselves to it. Jesus showed the importance of Scripture when He said, "Man does not live on bread alone, but on every word that comes from the mouth of God" (Matt. 4:4). We need to know it, and, as the apostle Paul instructs us, handle it correctly (2 Tim. 2:15). Thus far we have seen that

Jesus' ministry was incarnational and intentional. We now turn to one last principle.

Jesus' public ministry was inclusive; that is, He ministered to both the spiritual and social needs of people. Another word that would describe the ministry of Jesus is "wholistic [sic]."[126] The biblical record speaks for itself in regard to this issue. The gospel accounts portray for us a Christ who, while preparing people for eternity, did not ignore their needs in time. He was concerned about all that concerned them. Let us now consider these two aspects of our Lord's ministry.

Without question, Jesus was concerned about humanity's spiritual needs. As was stated earlier, He came to seek and save lost humanity (Luke 19:10). He attempted to reach people largely through His teaching and preaching. The gospels are replete with references to Jesus' ministry of teaching and preaching. A quick survey of the pages of the gospels in a red-letter edition of the New Testament will demonstrate how extensively Jesus gave Himself to these ministries. He spoke in the recognized houses of worship (Mark 1:21; Luke 4:16-22) in various locations (Matt. 4:23; Luke 4:15). He spoke in the open air to large crowds (Luke 6:17-18) and privately to His own disciples (Matt. 13:36-43). He gave individualized instruction to Nicodemus (John 3) and the woman at the well (John 4). No audience was too large or too small for Him. He gave Himself without reservation to the proclamation of the Word of God. He confronted sin and hypocrisy (Mark 7; Matt. 23), corrected spiritual misunderstandings, gave a full exposition of the truth of God (Matt. 5:17-48), and pointed the way to salvation (John 14:6). Few would deny that this was a major part of Jesus' ministry.

A less widely heralded, but nonetheless biblical, part of Jesus' ministry was directed toward the temporal needs of humanity. In one sense, we have seen some of this already. In the gospel accounts there are a number of texts which refer to physical healings that Jesus performed. Sometimes He healed large numbers of people at a given time (Matt. 8:16; 12:15); at other times He

---

[126] Villafané, 13.

healed individuals (Matt. 8:14-15; Mark 2:1-12). He ministered to all kinds of physical problems: leprosy (Matt. 8:1-4), paralysis (Matt. 9:1-8), blindness and the inability to speak (Matt. 9:27-34), bleeding (Matt. 9:20-22), a deformed limb (Matt. 12:9-14), and deafness (Mark 7:31-36). All of these things demonstrate a care for the body, but it doesn't stop there.

Jesus further showed His care for the temporal needs of humanity by providing food. On one occasion, He provided bread and fish for a crowd in excess of 5,000 people (Matt. 14:13-21). On another occasion, He provided the same meal for a crowd of over 4,000 people (Matt. 15:29-39). He also provided fish for His disciples and their fishing business (Luke 5:1-11). And on another occasion, He provided tax money for one of His disciples (Matt. 17:24-27). All of these things show Jesus' concern for the temporal needs of people, and all of these needs were supplied by supernatural means.

On a more practical level, Ron Sider calls our attention to the fact that Jesus and His disciples had a common purse out of which money was some-times taken and given to the poor (John 13:29).[127]

So, Jesus demonstrated by His life that He cared for the temporal needs of humanity. If His public ministry is a model for the public ministry of the church, and we have established that it is, the church should engage in similar activities.

In addition to His example, Jesus also provides His followers with clear instructions that ministering to temporal or social needs is a part of what they are to do. The Parable of the Good Samaritan (Luke 10:29-37) teaches the necessity of caring for our neighbors' health and well-being, even though they may not be like us, and it may cost us. The passage about the sheep and the goats in Matthew 25 specifically mentions meeting a number of physical or social needs, feeding the hungry, giving a drink to the thirsty, housing the stranger, giving clothes to the naked, and visiting those who are in prison (25:31-46). The seriousness of performing these ministries is seen in Jesus'

---

[127] Ron J. Sider, *Rich Christians in an Age of Hunger: Moving From Affluence to Generosity* (Dallas, TX: Word Publishing, 1997, 20th Anniversary Edition), 78.

response to those who neglected to help the needy; He casts them from His presence. As Ron Sider reminds us, those with abundance who do not feed the hungry and clothe the naked go to hell.[128] This is a very sobering thought and cause for great reflection by the church.

For too long there has been a division in the church. Some parts of the church have emphasized the evangelistic, or so called "spiritual" side of ministry, while other parts of the church have emphasized the social side of ministry. The evangelical church has tended to be part of the first group. The true biblical position is not either/or, but both. As Dr. Villafané writes, "The evangelical church is thus challenged to acknowledge that an authentic and relevant spirituality must be wholistic [sic] responding to both the vertical and horizontal dimensions of life."[129] John Stott puts it this way: "Thus social responsibility becomes an aspect not of Christian mission only, but also of Christian conversion. It is impossible to be truly converted to God...without being thereby converted to our neighbor."[130]

As Jesus' ministry was inclusive in content, it was also inclusive in contacts. Jesus ministered to men (Matt. 9:1-8; 20:29-34), women (Matt. 8:14-15; 9:20-22), and children (Mark 10:13-16). He engaged the religiously respectable (John 3) and the seemingly reprobate (Matt. 9:11; Luke 7:36-39). Jesus' ministry was not restricted by a person's gender, age, or moral character. He touched all kinds of people. But His outreach went even beyond this.

Of particular interest in this respect were the remarks of Wally Tilleman in a Saturday workshop on community organizing that was part of the course requirements for a Gordon-Conwell course on the public ministry of the church. He made reference to several individuals that Jesus ministered to in Matthew 8, specifically, the leper, the centurion, and the apostle Peter's mother-in-law. He noted that each of these were marginalized people in

---

[128] Ibid, preface, xiv.

[129] Villafané, 15.

[130] Stott, 53.

Jewish society. The leper was an outcast (Lev. 13:45-46), the centurion was probably a foreigner, and the woman was a "second-rate citizen." There was a certain stigma about getting involved with some of these people. Jesus was looked down upon because of some of the company that He kept (Matt. 9:11). But He kept their company unashamedly because they were His mission field (Matt. 9:13), and He needed to make contact with them in order to fulfill His mission (Luke 19:10). We, the church, need to be careful that we do not place restrictions on who we will minister to, for that contradicts the example and teaching of our Lord. He was a man for all people.

In this article we have looked at the ministry of Jesus Christ. We have seen the tasks that He gave Himself to, and have determined, based upon His teachings, that He intended these ministries to continue down through the ages through His body, the church. This study is not just good theology; it is our mission until He comes. In these pages we have also seen how Jesus conducted His ministry, through being present with people (through the incarnation), by engaging them (through intentionality), and by reaching out to all (being inclusive). His ministry was successful, impacting lives for time and for eternity. If we, as the church, hope to have a similar impact, we need to follow His example.

Chapter 15 The School of Faith
Text: Luke 8:40-56

Hebrews 11:1 defines faith as "being sure of what we hope for and certain of what we do not see." A few verses later, the author of Hebrews tells us how important faith is. He says, "And without faith it is impossible to please God, because anyone who comes to him must believe that he exists and that he rewards those who earnestly seek him (11:6)." So faith is vitally important. This truth is made plain not only from the verse in Hebrews that was just cited but also from the examples of many godly people in Scripture. Abraham believed God; Moses believed God; David believed God. In fact, pick almost any person that you admire in Scripture, and I dare say that they will be a person of faith.

As Christians, we know that we are saved by grace through faith in our Lord Jesus Christ (Eph. 2:8). But faith is not just for salvation. Faith is to affect all of our life. Habakkuk 2:4 says, "But the righteous will live by his faith." Paul also affirms this principle in the New Testament in Romans 1:17.

We all know that we should have faith and that it should control our lives, but if we are honest, we would confess that from time to time we struggle with the issue of faith. So how does one develop a strong faith? What does it look like?

All of us have probably had some degree of schooling. In school we all had some courses that we liked, and some that we didn't like. Maybe you did not like math. You just did not like memorizing multiplication tables. You struggled with them and at the time could not see the value of them; now, however, you see their usefulness. When you get your paycheck, you can easily tell if a mistake has been made by simply multiplying the number of hours that you worked by your hourly rate. So though you struggled with the subject, it has yielded some good results.

In the spiritual life, there are also lessons for us to learn, and not all of them are pleasant, but they are for our benefit and can strengthen us. Faith is one of the areas that we sometimes struggle with. Faith is grown through experience and challenge.

You perhaps think that I am going to speak about the woman with the issue of blood. She is most certainly an example of faith; however, I would like to have us focus our attention on Jairus. He too is an example of faith in this passage. In fact, I dare say that Jairus is an example of mature faith, and we can learn much from him.

By this time in Luke's gospel Jesus had established Himself as a healer and miracle worker. He had freed men from demon-possession (4:35; 8:26-33), healed Peter's mother-in-law of a fever (4:38-39), healed a man with leprosy (5:12-13), a man with a shriveled hand (6:6-10), a paralytic (5:17-25), a sick servant (7:1-10), raised a widow's son back to life (7:11-15), and healed some women of diseases and cured them of evil spirits (8:2). In addition to these individual miracles, we find various summary statements that indicate that Jesus did many miracles (4:40; 5:15; 6:17-18; 7:21).

Also by this time Jesus had received mixed reviews in the Jewish synagogues. He had been praised in the synagogue in Capernaum, rejected in the one in Nazareth, where they tried to kill Him, and they were furious with Him in the synagogue where He healed the man with the withered hand. He had succeeded in upsetting the Jewish religious leaders on a number of occasions (5:21,30,33; 6:2,7,11; 7:39).

So in one sense, it is a bit surprising to find Jairus, a synagogue ruler, coming to Jesus. We don't know if Jairus had been following Jesus' ministry or whether this was the first time that he had seen Him. In view of his office, he would be a man of standing in the community.[131] He may be jeopardizing his standing in the Jewish community by his actions in this passage of Scrip-

[131] Craig Keener, *The IVP Bible Background Commentary: New Testament* (Downers Grove, IL: InterVarsity Press, 1993), 211.

ture. But regardless of the circumstances, he comes to Jesus.

He had probably by this time heard that Jesus could heal and work miracles. The very fact that he comes to Jesus with his need indicates that he either has faith or is desperate. I suspect that it was probably a bit of both. The need that he has is an issue of life and death; his daughter's life is at stake. His faith is seen not only in his coming to Jesus with his need but also in the fact that he makes his way through the crowd in order to get to Jesus to secure His help. The text in Luke does not tell us what Jairus said when he came to Jesus. It only records some of the details of how he approached Jesus; we will look at these shortly.

In order to find out what Jairus said to Jesus, we need to consult the account of one of the other gospel writers. We will look at Mark's account. In Mark 5:23 we are told that Jairus said, "Please come and put your hands on her so that she will be healed and live." In this text Jairus expresses confidence in Jesus' ability to do what he is requesting. Faith ought to have confidence.

I heard of a case where a woman asked some other sisters in the church to pray for her regarding a specific need. When they were done praying and the condition was the same, the woman thanked the ladies for praying for her and then said, "I knew it wouldn't work." Faith ought to be expectant. James tells us in his epistle that when we ask for something from God we ought to ask in faith or we should not expect to receive anything from the Lord (Jas.1:6-7). Jesus also emphasized the importance of faith when He told people that their faith played a part in their healing (Matt. 9:22,29).

A second thing that I think is worth noting is the attitude in which Jairus approached Jesus. Verse 41 of the passage tells us that Jairus came to Jesus, fell at His feet, and pleaded with Jesus to come to his house. These words tell us something about the spirit in which Jairus approached Jesus. "Fell at his feet" can also be translated as "knelt."[132] The word can thus indicate worship,

---

[132] Paul R. McReynolds, ed., *Word Study Greek-English New Testament* (Wheaton, IL: Tyndale House Publishers, 1998), 1591-1592.

respect, and entreaty. The wise men who came to visit Jesus shortly after His birth did this (Matt. 2:11); a leper did this to Jesus in the gospels (Luke 5:12); John did this to Jesus on the Isle of Patmos (Rev. 1:17; 19:10; 22:8); and the twenty-four elders, four living creatures, and the angels did this in the Book of Revelation to both the Father and the Son.[133] Jairus came before Jesus with humility. Even as a person of standing in the community, he humbles himself, and that publicly before Jesus. The word *pleading* in our text also tells us something about Jairus' approach to Jesus. The word can be translated "begged."[134] There was an urgency in Jairus' request, but we should also note that Jairus came asking and not telling Jesus what to do. He did not perceive his request as a right.

It is unfortunate, but we have people in the church today who think that faith is commanding God to do things. This is a misunderstanding of faith. While faith is to include confidence, it is not to include arrogance. The Bible is very clear that God resists the proud but gives grace to the humble (Jas. 4:6). Our text is an illustration of this truth. Jairus came to Jesus with a humble and respectful faith, and Jesus honored that. He consented to go to Jairus' house. How happy Jairus must have been: the one whose help he hoped to secure was on the way to his house! But there was going to be another lesson in the school of faith for him. He was going to need more than a faith with a proper attitude; he was going to need a faith that could abide.

It is easy to believe when all is going well; this is not true, however, in adversity. As soon as Jesus starts to make His way to Jairus' house, there is trouble. The latter part of verse 41 tells us that as Jesus was on the way to Jairus' house the crowds almost crushed Him. Jesus and Jairus are in the midst of a large crowd. One thing about crowds is that they tend not to move very quickly. If you have ever tried to leave a major league stadium after a baseball game, then you know what I am talking about. But as if this were not enough, there is another problem. In verse 44 we find a woman with an issue of blood who comes up behind Jesus, touches the hem of His garment, and that stops everything. Jesus says, "Who touched me?" and evidently He was not going to move until He found out who had touched Him. The latter part of verse 45 tells us that everyone was denying it. So it seems that they stood right where they were as Jesus tried to find out who touched Him. Verse 47 tells us that when the woman saw that she could not go unnoticed, she told Jesus that she was the one who touched Him, and she told Him what had happened to her. So, she gave her testimony. You know how some people are about giving testimonies; they can be long-winded. The gospels don't tell us all that this woman said to Jesus, but just think about it for a minute. She had a long-standing medical condition that no doctors could heal (Mark 5:26), and now she is healed in an instant. She is going to have something to say. Even if she is not long-winded, she is probably choking back tears as she speaks, thus taking time.

Imagine for a moment that you are Jairus. You have an urgent need—a matter of life and death involving your twelve year old daughter, your only daughter. You have secured Jesus' attention in the matter; you have made slow progress toward your home because of the crowd; and now you are stuck on the road with this woman. How would you feel? Precious time is being wasted. What kinds of thoughts would run through your mind if you were Jairus? *This woman has had this condition for twelve years; couldn't she have waited another hour? Why does she have to stop us now? Besides, I asked Jesus for help first; let her wait her turn. On top of all this, I heard Jesus say that power had gone out from Him. Is He going to have enough power to meet the need that I have come to Him with? My need is big.* How do we handle it when our needs are as yet unmet and others who have sought God after us have their needs met first? Can we handle it? Can we endure delay? Handling delay is part of the maturing process.

In addition in our text, there is the issue of uncleanness.[135] This woman is

---

[135] Darrell L. Bock, *Luke Volume 1 1:1-9:50*, Baker Exegetical Commentary on the New Testament (Grand Rapids, MI: Baker Books, 1994), 793.

ceremonially unclean according to Old Testament law (Lev. 15:19-33).[136] By rights, she should not have been in this crowd. Here she publicly admits to being unclean and touching Jesus. As a synagogue ruler, do you now want this "unclean" Jesus in your good Jewish home? Oh, the emotional turmoil that Jairus may have had at this time. But this is nothing compared to what happened next. In verse 49 someone from Jairus' house shows up and tells Jairus that his daughter has died and that he shouldn't trouble the teacher anymore. This had to be the ultimate blow. Jairus must have been crushed, but Jesus speaks a word of encouragement to him. In verse 50 Jesus says "Don't be afraid; just believe, and she will be healed." Now Jesus had already raised one person from the dead earlier in the gospel. He raised the son of the widow of Naim in Luke 7. So Jesus has a reliable track record in this area. However, it is somehow harder to have faith for your own particular need. This being the case, Jesus speaks directly to Jairus concerning his daughter. Jesus knows how to encourage us to go a little bit further when we feel that we have no strength. Jairus believes Jesus and continues on to his house with Him. Jairus has approached Jesus with a proper attitude and has abided with Him in the midst of delay and disaster, and he is going to receive an answer to his request on behalf of his daughter.

In verse 52 we find that when Jesus gets to the house the musicians and mourners are there. This was customary in the ancient world. In fact, some of those who mourned would be professional mourners brought in for the occasion.[137] The signs of death and hopelessness are everywhere. The air is charged with grief. This is a great travesty, not only because the girl is young, but also because she was approaching the age for marriage, and now it seems she will never be married.[138] From a purely human point of view, the situation is impossible; it is irreversible. Death has arrived.

"Stop wailing," Jesus said, "she is not dead but asleep" (Luke 8:52). After

[136] Keener, 211.

[137] Ibid, 212.

[138] Ibid, 149.

He said this, those who were gathered there laugh at Him. It is as though they are saying to Him, "Jesus, You are not facing reality here; we have seen death before, and this girl is dead. There is nothing more that can be done."

I wonder how Jairus felt then. Back in verse 50 Jesus had tried to encourage him, telling him not to be afraid but to believe and his daughter will be healed; now the majority is telling him it is over. What can we do then when the money is running out and our lives are coming apart spiritually, physically, and emotionally? We can do what Jairus did and stay close to Jesus to see what He will do.

Jairus stays right with Jesus. What other alternative does he have? There are really not any other options for him to regain his daughter. And even though it may seem like an outside chance, it is the only one that he has. He is pressed to one option. God will sometimes allow similar circumstances in our lives.

Jairus, his wife, Jesus, and Peter, James, and John go in to where the girl is. Jesus takes her by the hand and tells her to get up—and she does. Jairus receives a miracle. But the miracle he received was greater than the one that he came to Jesus for. He came to Jesus seeking healing for his daughter. He wound up seeing her raised from the dead. He had a greater revelation of God's power. God sometimes seems to let things get worse before they get better. This is unpleasant; it stretches us, it tests our faith, but it can have great value. We can have a greater revelation of God, and the experience can mature us. This is part of the program in the "school of faith." And we find that, here too, God is faithful. When He says that He is going to do something, He makes good on it.

What can we learn from the experience of Jairus? We can learn a number of things. First, we can see that faith is not merely intellectual assent; it is something that is to be lived out in the practical human experiences of life. The second thing that we can learn is that the faith that God delights in has a number of components to it: it is expectant, humble, and perseverant. As we face life and all that it throws at us, we need to realize that our faith will be tested, and that we too will be students in the school of faith for our entire life. Since this is the case, go to Jesus and stay with Him. The Book of Hebrews tells us that He is the "author and perfecter of our faith..." (Heb. 12:2).

Chapter 16 Beyond Conversion

Discipling New Converts From Paul's Thessalonian Letters

The church of Jesus Christ has been entrusted with the great privilege and responsibility of proclaiming the gospel to the world (Mark 16:15; Matt. 28:19-20). This commission is in keeping with God's plan and purpose (Matt. 24:14; 2 Pet. 3:9). The charge to evangelize is a privilege in that when the church speaks for her Lord, the Lord speaks through His church (2 Cor. 5:20), offering a lost humanity reconciliation with their maker. The evangelistic task is a responsibility in that the Lord has commanded the church to carry it out and many peoples' eternal destiny, in part, depends upon our faithfulness in this ministry. Thus, we dare not shirk this responsibility.

When the gospel is preached, the hearers will either accept it or reject it; there is no middle ground. We rejoice with those who accept the Lord, and rightfully so; they have received the gift of eternal life (John 3:16), become part of the family of God (Gal. 6:10), and caused rejoicing in Heaven (Luke 15:7,10). However, the church's responsibility is not fulfilled by bringing people to Jesus Christ. As important as conversion is, it is only the beginning. The church also has the responsibility to mold the new convert into a dedicated disciple of Jesus Christ. In Matthew 28, the Lord lays that task squarely on the shoulders of the church.

The question may be raised, what is a disciple? Jesus describes His disciples as those who love Him more than anyone else (Matt. 10:37; Luke 14:26), who carry their cross (Luke 14:27), hold to His teaching (John 8:31), love one another (John 13:34), and are fruitful (John 15:8). The Great Commission passage in Matthew 28 would add to this list that a disciple is one who is baptized and is instructed to obey everything that Jesus Christ commands. Thus, a disciple is one who is thoroughly committed to Jesus

Christ, as evidenced by their faithfulness and fruitfulness. This is a tall order; in fact, it is a life-long task.

But how do we take a new convert and mold him or her into such a disciple? Well, certainly we need people who are "good soil" (Mark 4:20), and we also need the help of the Holy Spirit. But what type of instruction and guidance can we give to the new convert to root and ground him in the faith and get him started along the path to spiritual maturity? Fortunately, the New Testament provides us with an apostolic answer to these questions. These answers are found in Paul's letters to the young church in Thessalonica.

The church in Thessalonica was founded by the apostle Paul on his second missionary journey; the account of its beginning is found in Acts 17:1-9. The Acts account is very brief and doesn't supply us with much detail about the early days of the church there. But Paul's two letters to the Thessalonians do fill us in on some important information regarding the early days of the gospel in that city. What is particularly significant about the Thessalonian letters is that some scholars feel that they are among the earliest New Testament documents; as such they provide us with very early information about what was done to disciple new converts. Another factor that makes the study of Paul's discipleship methods among the Thessalonians interesting is the remarkable spiritual progress of these new converts.

The spiritual progress of the Thessalonian Christians can be seen in the commendations that Paul gives to them. In First Thessalonians 1:3, Paul acknowledges the presence of faith, hope, and love in their lives. Warren Wiersbe says, "Faith, hope, and love are the three cardinal virtues of the Christian life, and the three greatest evidences of salvation."[139] John Stott writes, "Faith, hope, and love sound rather abstract qualities, but they have concrete, practical results."[140] Paul knew that the Thessalonians possessed

---

[139] Warren W. Wiersbe, *Be Ready* (Wheaton, IL: Victor Books, 1984), 26.

[140] John Stott, *The Gospel & the End of Time* (Downers Grove, IL: InterVarsity Press, 1991), 30.

these qualities because they were made manifest by their work, labor, and endurance (1 Thess. 1:3). First Thessalonians 1:8 indicates that they were very evangelistic. Their witness made an impact not only on their own country but also beyond its borders. In verse 7 Paul says that the Thessalonians were model Christians; that is, they were a good example for other believers to follow. Leon Morris says, "This is high praise, for in the first place Paul calls no other church a pattern, and in the second he thinks of them as examples, not only to heathen, but to Christians throughout Greece."[141] Coming from a man with such high standards, this is indeed high praise. In Second Thessalonians 1:3, he acknowledges their continual growth in faith and love. They are truly standing firm in their new faith (1 Thess. 3:8). This is exceptional progress when one considers that they are undergoing persecution (1 Thess. 1:6; 2:14; 3:3-4; 2 Thess. 1:6) and that they do not have their spiritual father, Paul, personally with them to assist them in their spiritual walk. The Thessalonian Christians are blossoming under less than ideal circumstances. Let us turn our attention now to how the apostle discipled them.

The first area that I would like to give attention to is Paul's early instructions to the infant church in Thessalonica, things that he taught them while he was still with them. John Stott calls attention to some of these early teachings.[142] We are going to look at them and others below. We can determine what some of these teachings were from the passages in Paul's letters where he makes reference to having told them certain things (1 Thess. 3:4; 4:1,6,11; 2 Thess. 2:5) or their knowing certain things (1 Thess. 4:2; 5:2; 2 Thess. 3:7). Both refer to previous instruction. Let us now look more closely at the substance of these early instructions.

In First Thessalonians 3:4, Paul tells us that he taught his new converts that they would be persecuted. In fact, the text indicates that he emphasized this point again and again. John Stott says, "It is very interesting to learn that

[141] Leon Morris, *The Epistles of Paul to the Thessalonians*. Tyndale New Testament Commentaries (Grand Rapids, MI: Wm. B. Eerdman Publishing Company, 1976), 38.
[142] Stott, 77.

a regular topic of Paul's instruction to converts was the inevitability of suffering."[143] Nowadays, at least in America, this teaching is largely neglected. Part of the reason for this may be that we are not presently suffering persecution. Another possible reason is that we don't want to tell people that the faith that they have embraced could bring them troubles; this is especially true of new converts. But the apostle Paul did not shrink back from telling his converts this truth. Believers are in the world but are not to be of it. Being different can cause conflict; in fact, elsewhere in the New Testament Paul said that it would (2 Tim. 3:12). Thus, in telling the Thessalonians that they would be persecuted, Paul is painting them a very realistic picture of what they can expect now that they are Christians. Hostility to the gospel still exists today, and as we seek to share the good news in obedience to our Lord (Matt. 28:19), we can expect to encounter some of that hostility. Warren Wiersbe says, "We must warn new believers that the way is not easy as they seek to live for Christ; otherwise, when trials come, these babes in Christ will be discouraged and defeated."[144] New Christians need to be instructed about this in order to be prepared for it. Avoiding the subject of persecution is misrepresenting the teachings of Christ and the apostles. While we may be afraid to tell people that they will be persecuted, for fear that they will walk away from the Lord, failing to tell them may produce the same result. In counting the cost, believers need to be able to do so based on truth; Paul gave them the truth.

As we move further into the Thessalonian correspondence, we find Paul dealing with some very practical issues of Christian living. In First Thessalonians 4:1-2, Paul speaks in very general terms about having instructed the Thessalonians in how to live a life that is pleasing to God. In the verses that follow, he gives some concrete examples of what that entails. The first one deals with sexual behavior. Paul urges the Thessalonians to abstain from sexual immorality. This was a much needed word then (as it is now), in view

---

[143] Stott, 65.

[144] Wiersbe, 62.

of the culture in which they lived. Craig Keener has pointed out, "Unmarried Greek men (i.e., Greek men below the age of thirty) commonly indulged in intercourse with prostitutes, slaves and other males; Greek religion and culture did not provide any disincentive for doing so."[145] Greek society as a whole was charged with sexual immorality, and this included Thessalonica. This being the case, Paul addressed them on the subject of sexual relations, and gave them God's perspective on it. God's will is self control. God is the one who created human sexuality, and He also set down the principles governing its proper expression. As someone has said, God's standard is that sex is to take place only between a man and a woman who are married to each other. The consequences for violating this standard are severe (see verse 6). Instructions such as this need to be repeated again and again; new converts need to understand what sin is. They also need to know that Christians are to be a different people who do not take their cues from the world but from the Word of God. It does not matter that "everybody else is doing it"; the believer's first task is to please God, and he or she can do so by living in a manner which is consistent with God's character, namely, purity.

The next passage that I would like to have us consider is First Thessalonians 4:11. In this text, we learn some positive instructions that Paul gave to the Thessalonians when he was with them; that is, some things that he said should be a part of their lives. The Christian life is not just a list of "thou shalt nots"; it also contains some "thou shalts." This particular "thou shalt" is "thou shalt work." This seemingly secular practice is very important and has spiritual significance; thus, Paul urges the Thessalonians to work. The reason is that the Christian's work, or lack of it, sends a message to the unbelieving world. Paul wanted the Thessalonians to send a good message to their neighbors. At the time Paul wrote First Thessalonians, it seems that some in the church had stopped working; Paul writes and reminds them that they need to work. Work is generally a part of one's public life, and neighbors, friends,

---

[145] Craig S. Keener, *The IVP Bible Background Commentary: New Testament* (Downers Grove, IL: InterVarsity Press, 1993), 590.

and others in the community see what is done. Unbelievers don't see how Christians sing or pray in church because they don't go to church meetings. But, they do see how believers live on the job and in the community. Thus, the Christian needs to be careful to present a life that glorifies God in every way (1 Cor. 10:31). Being industrious glorifies God. We are a watched people. Unfortunately, some in the Thessalonian church didn't heed Paul's instruction, and he had to bring up the subject again in his second letter (2 Thess. 3:6-8). We will look at that passage a little bit later.

Another subject that Paul covered in his instruction of new converts was eschatology, or last things. He makes reference to this in First Thessalonians 5:1-2 and Second Thessalonians 2:1-5 (First Thessalonians 4:6, which was mentioned earlier, would also fall under this category). Concerning First Thessalonians 5:1, Leon Morris writes, "His first point is that they really have no need for instruction in the matter of the time. He had spoken of this in his first preaching, and evidently counted on this as having been well learned at the time, so that he had no need to write on the topic." [146] This along with the above-mentioned text in Second Thessalonians 2 suggests a rather substantial eschatological instruction. Now it is true that the Thessalonians had some questions and misunderstandings about some issues, as evidenced by First Thessalonians 4:13-18 and Second Thessalonians 2:1-3, but the teaching that they received in the early days was profitable to them nonetheless. To begin with, it gave them an awareness of where this world is headed. God has a plan that He is working; it may be somewhat veiled from our eyes, but it will certainly come to pass. His plan includes the overthrow of wickedness, the judgment of sin, and the rewarding of the saints. Awareness of such truths can provide an appreciation for salvation in Christ, an incentive to guard one's life so as not to lose our inheritance, and a burden to witness to those who are not yet saved. Some of these truths would also be an encouragement to the Thessalonians who were being persecuted for their faith.

These texts that we have looked at in the letters to the Thessalonians

[146] Morris, 89-90.

show us that Paul's early instruction of the believers there gave them a framework in which to understand their new-found faith. He outlined for them how the world would treat them, how they were to live in the world, and where this world is headed. Paul was a man of great wisdom and insight, and his teaching seems to have been effective in rooting and grounding this church in the faith—for it was growing in the midst of persecution and that in the absence of the apostle Paul.

Paul's discipling of his new converts was not limited to his words but also included his ways, that is, how he lived among them. His example was one from which they could learn. The way that he lived among them contributed in a positive way to the message that he preached, for he practiced what he preached. This consistency is absolutely vital. Warren Wiersbe writes, "A Christian leader may appeal to the authority of the Word; but if he cannot point also to his own example of obedience, his people will not listen." [147] As we saw earlier, Paul instructed the Thessalonian Christians to work, but he also served as a model for them (1 Thess. 2:9; 2 Thess. 3:7-8). The same holds true regarding other matters of Christian living. In First Thessalonians 4, Paul declared that it is God's will that His people be sanctified or holy. In the second chapter of the same letter, he points to his own holiness which he says that both God and the Thessalonians can verify (1 Thess. 2:10). In First Thessalonians 3:12, Paul prayed that God would cause their love to increase and overflow for others in the same fashion that Paul and his companions' love overflowed toward them. The love of Paul for the Thessalonians can be seen in a special way in the second chapter of this same letter. There Paul is seen among them as gentle, encouraging, and comforting, even giving each of them individual attention. In First Thessalonians 2:8, he plainly declares his love for them. He shared his message and his life with them.

The gospel message needs to be shared, but it also needs to be seen, fleshed out in the lives of God's people. Paul blended together in beautiful harmony his words and his ways and thus presented a compelling gospel.

---

[147] Wiersbe, 168.

New converts need to see how the Christian life is lived. There is some truth to the old adage that "a picture is worth a thousand words." May Paul's consistency between his message and his life be an inspiration and example to those of us who attempt to disciple new converts and bring them beyond conversion.

In closing, there is one last thing that I would like to say about Paul's early teaching of the believers in Thessalonica. We do not know the exact length of time that Paul spent with the new converts there. We do know that the church was started in somewhat turbulent times (see Acts 17:1-8). In view of this fact and the possibility that he might have to leave the city quickly at any time, he proceeded to instruct the new believers in things of primary importance: the place of persecution in the Christian life, holiness, and eschatology. In view of the spiritual fortitude and progress that the Thessalonian Christians had, we will do well to consider Paul's methods as we seek to build disciples who are faithful and fruitful.

Chapter 17 Model Christians

I once heard the word model defined as "a cheap imitation of the real thing." That is a valid definition in certain contexts. If you go into a hobby shop, you will probably find a section of model airplanes, cars, and boats. These plastic replicas look similar to the genuine articles, but they are much smaller, more fragile, and less costly than the originals. They also do not perform all the functions of the original. They are, in fact, "cheap imitations of the real thing."

When we attach the word *model* to a Christian, we do not want it to be understood in the way just mentioned. Rather, by model Christian, we mean one who is exemplary, worth imitating, a good example. As believers in Christ, we must be good examples.

When one of my sons was very young, people would on occasion say, "he looks just like you," or "you can tell who his father is." He had no choice in the resemblance that he bears; it was his by birth. The similarities that we share are not limited to our faces. It has also been noted that he stands like me; that is, he puts his arms in the same position as I do when standing. This resemblance he did not inherit by birth, but learned by observing me. Now, copying my mannerisms will probably not radically affect his future, but it serves to illustrate the point that the young imitate what they see in those who are older. We cannot deny the fact that the young are impressionable. This same principle holds true in the church; younger Christians look to those who have been in the faith longer as examples.

Example is a powerful teacher. When I was in Bible school, one of my instructors made this statement, "Your actions speak so loud I can't hear what you say." That statement indicates that people are affected more by what we do than what we say. Actions often do speak louder than words. The role models that a person chooses can profoundly affect his or her life. Timothy, Paul's associate, had a godly mother and grandmother. I can't help but think that their example, plus that of the apostle Paul, served to set Timothy on a godly course.

The apostle Paul understood the value of godly models; thus, he wrote and instructed others to follow or imitate him (1 Cor. 4:16; 11:1; Phil. 3:7; 2 Thess. 3:7-9). That is not a statement that one should make lightly, and I'm sure Paul did not. Holding yourself out as an example to follow carries tremendous responsibility. Now Paul was not claiming sinless perfection for himself; in First Corinthians 11:1, he encourages the Corinthians to follow him as he follows the example of Christ. But Paul was of sufficient maturity to hold out his life as an example to follow. The question that we might ask ourselves is: Would we feel comfortable encouraging others to imitate us? I once heard an older Christian brother share some words that he said he has never forgotten. When he was in the military, his chaplain said, "You are the best Christian that somebody knows." That is a sobering thought. Are we a good representation of one who professes faith in Christ? We may be good compared to others, but compared to the principles of God's Word, how do we measure up? If we are diligent and consistent in our walk with Christ, we can be at rest if others follow our example. But if not, we cannot afford to say, "Do as I say, not as I do." We need to change. Not only for our own sake, but also for the good of those who may look to us as examples.

The importance of being a model Christian can be seen in First Thessalonians 1. In verses 4 through 9, Paul gives a brief history of the coming of the gospel to Thessalonica. As he records the early days of his ministry in the city, he makes several statements related to the subject of being an example. In verse 5 he refers to how he and his companions lived among the Thessalonians. In the second chapter of the epistle, verses 1 through 12, Paul gives us some of the details of how they conducted themselves among the believers there. This passage tells us that they were hard working, people of integrity, holy, blameless, persevering, and loving. We must keep these things in mind, because in First Thessalonians 1:6 Paul says that the Thessalonian believers became imitators of him and his coworkers and of the Lord. These new converts were very impressionable, and Paul's life and faith greatly influenced their lives. By observing him, they learned how to live a quality Christian life, even in the face of persecution. Paul set a good example for them. The importance of this becomes apparent when we consider Paul's words in First Thessalonians 1:7, where he tells us that the Thessalonians became examples to all the believers in Macedonia and Achaia. The Thessalonians having learned how to live from Paul now were giving others an example to follow. As Leon Morris has written, "The imitators in their turn were imitated."[148] What we see emerging in these verses is a pattern wherein faith is communicated by life. People imitate what they see. That is what makes it so vitally important that we live lives worthy of the Lord, because others may be watching and following our example. If our lives do not reflect a firm commitment to Christ, we are in danger of reproducing Christians after our likeness, Christians who are living below the standard of what God desires.

While it is true that believers should follow the Lord and not other people, it is also true that those who are younger in the faith look for practical examples of what it means to follow Christ. They look for these practical examples in the lives of those who have known the Lord longer than they have. May we be model Christians who help others walk in His steps.

---

[148] Leon Morris, *The First and Second Epistles to the Thessalonians*, New International Commentary on the New Testament (Grand Rapids, MI: Wm. B. Eerdmans Publishing, 1959), 59.

Chapter 18 Being a Barnabas

The name Barnabas has come to be associated with encouragement; the reason for this is found in Acts 4:36. In this verse Luke, the writer of Acts, tells us that the name Barnabas means "Son of Encouragement." What is interesting is that Barnabas was not the given name of the man whom we have come to know by this name. The man's given name was Joseph (see Acts 4:36). The apostles called him Barnabas, and the name apparently stuck because he is referred to by that name every other time that he is mentioned in the New Testament. The name Joseph seems to fall by the wayside. The reason that the apostles called him Barnabas was probably because they saw the ministry of encouragement active in his life; it was a significant part of what he did.

According to *Strong's Exhaustive Concordance of the Bible: Greek Dictionary of the New Testament* the word translated as "encouragement" means, among other things, "exhortation" or "comfort."[149] These are uplifting kinds of words; "encouragement" is a very positive thing. As the people of God, we are engaged in conflict, conflict with the larger culture that does not hold our values, and conflict with the spiritual forces of darkness (Eph. 6:12) that would seek to discourage and destroy us. The people of God definitely need encouragement. It is one of the things that can help to preserve us in the midst of the downward pull that we all from time to time experience. It is also one of the purposes for which we are to gather together as the people of God (Heb.10:25). The church should not be, as someone has said, a place "where seldom is heard an encouraging word."

---

[149]James Strong, *Strong's Exhaustive Concordance of the Bible: Greek Dictionary of the New Testament* (Nashville, TN: Abington, 1978), 55.

There are some people in the church who have been specially gifted by God to be encouragers (Rom. 12:8). When I was in seminary, I had a professor with this gift. I describe him to others as "Barnabas incarnate"; encouragement just flowed from him; in fact, in the church he serves, his ministry is "Pastor of Encouragement." Encouragement is a ministry that is very important for Christian leaders to have. There are many verses in the New Testament that speak of Christian leaders encouraging others (the Book of 2 Timothy; Acts 11:23; 1 Thess. 3:2; Titus 2:6). This being said, encourage-ment is not something reserved for the specially gifted or for leaders. Paul instructs all Christians to participate in the ministry of encouragement (1 Thess. 4:18; 5:11). Thus, while a bubbling, outgoing personality might be helpful for one to be an encourager, we cannot excuse ourselves from parti-cipating in the ministry of encouragement based on our personality type. Paul would not have given a directive to all believers to encourage one another if it were not possible for them to do so. We all need to receive encouragement from time to time, and we all need to give it as well. So how can we be encouragers? How can we be a "Barnabas?" What are the traits of one who is an encourager? In order to answer these questions, let us look at the life of Barnabas.

In Acts 4:37 we learn that Barnabas sold a field that he owned and brought the money that he had received from the sale and laid it at the apostles' feet. Barnabas was a giving person. The first characteristic of an encourager is that they are generous; they desire to serve. In this particular case, Barnabas was generous with his resources, but being generous may take other forms; we may be called to be generous with our time. A "Barn-abas" is one who models the example of Jesus in that they come to serve, not to be served (Mark 10:45). They are people who are givers, willing to give of themselves and of their resources.

In Acts 9, we find another characteristic of an encourager; an encourager is one who is willing to stand up for people that others might not want anything to do with. In Acts 9, Saul of Tarsus, who had come to believe in

Jesus, tried to join himself to the church, and no one believed that he was a true disciple. Barnabas took him to the apostles and explained to them how Saul had met the Lord on the road and had now become a believer. Barnabas believed the best about Saul, and he was willing to take a risk for him. Barnabas was a man who was respected by the apostles, and so his speaking up for Saul opened a door for him that he would not have been able to open for himself. This is a good characteristic to have. However, this does not mean that we are to be totally indiscriminant. For example, if a person with a history of theft gets saved and starts to attend church that does not mean that we should immediately place them in positions where we know that they have exhibited failure or weakness before. We must use wisdom.

In Acts 11, we find another characteristic of an encourager. In this chapter we learn that some of the believers who left Jerusalem due to the persecution that arose after the stoning of Stephen went to Phoenicia, Cyprus, and Antioch. Some of the disciples from Cyprus and Cyrene started to share the gospel with Greeks. When the church in Jerusalem heard about this, they sent Barnabas to the church in Antioch. Barnabas, who was Jewish, was sent to a predominantly Gentile church. The Book of Acts, as well as the Book of Galatians shows us that the acceptance of non-Jewish people into the church was a thorny issue in the early days of the church.

Some believed that Gentiles should be accepted as true believers in Christ without being required to adhere to certain Jewish practices, such as circumcision. Others were insistent that Gentile Christians must submit to Jewish customs. The first church council, found in Acts 15, was called to discuss this very issue. What would Barnabas do when he got to Antioch?

Acts 11:23 tells us what Barnabas' reaction was. Luke writes, "When he arrived and saw the evidence of the grace of God, he was glad and encouraged them all to remain true to the Lord with all their hearts." Barnabas was able to affirm people who were different from himself and rejoice in what God was doing in their lives. Sometimes we have a hard time with this in the church today. We are uncomfortable with people who are ethnically or denominationally different than we are, and we allow these things to become barriers. Being a "Barnabas" will require us to overcome some of these hang-ups. The barriers that sometimes keep us apart are not supposed to. Galatians 3:28 says, "There is neither Jew nor Greek, slave nor free, male nor female, for you are all one in Christ Jesus." The Book of Revelation also affirms this truth. The company of believers found in the presence of God are people from every nation, tribe, people, and language (Rev. 7:9). We, in the present time, are to accept those whom God has accepted (Rom. 15:7).

Another characteristic of Barnabas' life was that he took a genuine interest in people's spiritual health and progress. The church needs people like this, particularly more mature believers who can strengthen and mentor younger believers. We see this also in Barnabas' life. Barnabas was a Christian before Paul was. The two of them were paired together in ministry in Acts 11:25-26 and on the first missionary journey that began in Acts 13. While it is true that Paul was an exceptional person, it is reasonable to assume that Barnabas was able, in some way, to mentor Paul and help him develop in his gifting. The church needs people who are willing to do this, to work with others and help them along.

As we look back over the list of the things that were characteristic of Barnabas' life—being a giving person, seeking to help one that others shunned, being able to work with people who were different from himself, and fostering the spiritual growth of others—we see that all of these qualities were good. In fact, more than good, they were Christ-like. May we seek to follow in the steps of Barnabas as he followed in the steps of Christ.

Bibliography

Bakke, Ray. *A Theology as Big as the City*. Downers Grove, IL: InterVarsity Press, 1997.

Barrett, C.K. *The First Epistle to the Corinthians*. Harper's New Testament Commentaries. New York: Harper & Row, 1968. Reprint, Peabody, MA: Hendrickson, 1987.

_____. *The Pastoral Epistles*. The New Clarendon Bible. London: Oxford University Press, 1963. Reprint, Grand Rapids, MI: Outreach Publications, 1986.

Beck, James R., and Craig L. Blomberg, eds. *Two Views on Women in Ministry*. Counterpoints. Grand Rapids, MI: Zondervan, 2001.

Bennett, Dennis, and Rita Bennett. *The Holy Spirit and You: A Study-Guide to the Spirit-Filled Life*. Plainfield, NJ: Logos International, 1971.

Bilezikian, Gilbert. *Community 101*. Grand Rapids, MI: Zondervan/Willow Creek Resources, 1997.

Bock, Darrell L. *Luke Volume 1 1:1-9:50*. Baker Exegetical Commentary on the New Testament. Grand Rapids, MI: Baker Books, 1994.

Brumback, Carl. *What Meaneth This?* Springfield, MO: Gospel Publishing House, 1947.

Burgess, Stanley, and Gary McGee, eds. *Dictionary of Pentecostal and Charismatic Movements*. Grand Rapids, MI: Zondervan, 1988.

Cook, Jerry, with Stanley Baldwin. *Love, Acceptance & Forgiveness*. Ventura, CA: Regal Books, 1979.

Cox, Harvey. *Fire From Heaven: The Rise of Pentecostal Spirituality and the Reshaping of Religion in the Twenty-First Century*. Reading, MA: Addison- Wesley Publishing, 1995.

Davis, John Jefferson. *Handbook of Basic Bible Texts: Every Key Passage for the Study of Doctrine and Theology*. Grand Rapids, MI: Zondervan/Academic, 1984.

Deere, Jack. *Surprised by the Power of the Spirit*. Grand Rapids, MI: Zondervan, 1993.

Fee, Gordon D. *The First Epistle to the Corinthians*. The New International Commentary on the New Testament. Grand Rapids, MI: Wm. B. Eerdmans, 1987.

_____. *God's Empowering Presence: The Holy Spirit in the Letters of Paul*. Peabody, MA: Hendrickson Publishers, 1994.

_____. *Gospel and Spirit: Issues in New Testament Hermeneutics*. Peabody, MA: Hendrickson Publishers, 1991.

_____. *Paul, The Spirit, and the People of God*. Peabody, MA: Hendrickson, 1996.

_____. *1 and 2 Timothy, Titus*. NIBC. Rev. ed. Peabody, MA: Hendrickson Publishers/Carlisle, Cumbria: Paternoster Press, 1995.

Fee, Gordon, and Douglas Stuart. *How to Read the Bible for All It's Worth: A Guide to Understanding the Bible*. Rev. ed. Grand Rapids, MI: Zondervan, 1993.

Ferguson, Everett. *Backgrounds of Early Christianity*. 2nd ed. Grand Rapids, MI: Wm. B. Eerdmans, 1993.

Gee, Donald. *Concerning Spiritual Gifts*. Rev. ed. Springfield, MO: Gospel Publishing House, 1972.

_____. *Spiritual Gifts in the Work of the Ministry Today*. Springfield, MO: Gospel Publishing House, 1963.

Goldsworthy, Graeme. *Prayer and the Knowledge of God*. Leicester, England: InterVarsity Press, 2003.

Grudem, Wayne A., ed. *Are Miraculous Gifts for Today? Four Views*. Counterpoints. Grand Rapids, MI: Zondervan, 1996.

Hodge, Charles. *Systematic Theology*. Edward N. Gross, ed. Abridged ed. Grand Rapids, MI: Baker Book House, 1988.

Hummel, Charles E. *Fire in the Fireplace: Contemporary Charismatic Renewal*. Downers Grove, IL: InterVarsity Press, 1978.

Keener, Craig S. *Gift & Giver: The Holy Spirit for Today*. Grand Rapids, MI: Baker Academic, 2001.

_____. *Paul, Women & Wives: Marriage and Women's Ministry in the Letters of Paul*. Peabody, MA: Hendrickson Publishers, 1992.

_____. *The IVP Bible Background Commentary: New Testament*. Downers Grove, IL: InterVarsity Press, 1993.

_____. *3 Crucial Questions About the Holy Spirit*. 3 Crucial Questions Series. Grand Rapids, MI: Baker Books, 1996.

Kendall, R.T. Vision statement. Online http://www.rtkendallministries.com (accessed May 2009).

Kent, Homer A., Jr. *The Pastoral Epistles: Studies in 1 and 2 Timothy and Titus*. Rev. ed. Chicago, IL: Moody Press, 1982.

Kostenberger, Andreas J., Thomas R. Schreiner, H. Scott Baldwin, eds. *Women in the Church: A Fresh Analysis of 1 Timothy 2:9-15*. Grand Rapids, MI: Baker Books, 1995.

Linthicum, Robert C. *Empowering the Poor: Community Organizing Among the City's 'Rag, Tag and Bobtail.'* Monrovia, CA: MARC/World Vision International, 1991.

MacArthur, John F., Jr. *Charismatic Chaos*. Grand Rapids, MI: Zondervan, 1992.

McReynolds, Paul R., ed. *Word Study Greek-English New Testament*. Wheaton, IL: Tyndale House Publisher, 1999.

Morris, Leon. *The Epistles of Paul to the Thessalonians*. Tyndale New Testament Commentaries. Grand Rapids, MI: Wm. B. Eerdmans Publishing Company, 1976.

_____. *The First Epistle of Paul to the Corinthians: An Introduction and Commentary*. The Tyndale New Testament Commentaries. Reprint, Leicester, England: InterVarsity / Grand Rapids, MI: Wm. B. Eerdmans, 1983.

_____. *The First and Second Epistles to the Thessalonians*. New International Commentary on the New Testament. Grand Rapids, MI: Wm. B. Eerdmans Publishing Company, 1959.

Sider, Ron J. *Rich Christians in an Age of Hunger: Moving From Affluence to Generosity*. Dallas, TX: Word Publishing, 1997.

Stott, John R. W. *Christian Mission in the Modern World*. Downers Grove, IL: InterVarsity Press, 1975.

_____. *The Gospel & the End of Time*. Downers Grove, IL: InterVarsity Press, 1991.

Strong, James. *Strong's Exhaustive Concordance of the Bible: Greek Dictionary of the New Testament*. Nashville, TN: Abington, 1978.

The Definition of Chalcedon, http://www.reformed.org/documents/index.html?mainframe=http://www.reformed.org /documents/chalcedon.html (accessed July 2010).

The Nicene Creed, http://www.reformed.org/documents/index.html (accessed June 2009).

Villafané, Eldin. *Seek the Peace of the City: Reflections on Urban Ministry*. Grand Rapids, MI: Wm. B. Eerdmans Publishing Company, 1995.

Wagner, C. Peter. *Your Spiritual Gifts Can Help Your Church Grow*. Glendale, CA: Regal Books, G/L Publications, 1979.

Warfield, Benjamin B. *Counterfeit Miracles*. New York: Charles Scribner's Sons, 1918.

_____. *The Person and Work of Christ*. Phillipsburg, NJ: Presbyterian and Reformed Publishing Company, 1950.

White, Randy. *Journey to the Center of the City: Making a Difference in an Urban Neighborhood*. Downers Grove, IL: InterVarsity Press, 1996.

Wiersbe, Warren W. *Be Ready*. Wheaton, IL: Victor Books, 1984.

Wight, Fred H. *Manners and Customs of Bible Lands*. Chicago, IL: Moody Press, 1953.

Williams, Don. *The Apostle Paul & Women in the Church*. Glendale, Ca: Regal Books, G/L Publications, 1977.

Winter, Bruce W. *After Paul Left Corinth: The Influence of Secular Ethics and Social Change*. Grand Rapids, MI: Wm. B. Eerdmans, 2001.

Witherington, Ben, III. *Conflict & Community in Corinth: A Socio-Rhetorical Commentary on 1 and 2 Corinthians*. Grand Rapids, MI: Wm. B. Eerdmans / Carlisle, Cumbria: Paternoster, 1995.

_____. *The Jesus Quest: The Third Search for the Jew of Nazareth*. 2nd ed. Downers Grove, IL: InterVarsity Press, 1997.

www.ingramcontent.com/pod-product-compliance
Lightning Source LLC
Chambersburg PA
CBHW051837040426
42447CB00006B/583